CU00661345

Victoria's Railway King

Victoria's Railway King

Sir Edward Watkin, One of the Victorian Era's Greatest Entrepreneurs and Visionaries

Geoffrey Scargill

FRONTLINE BOOKS

First published in Great Britain in 2021 by
Frontline Books
An imprint of
Pen & Sword Books Ltd
Yorkshire – Philadelphia

Copyright © Geoffrey Scargill, 2021

ISBN 978 1 52679 277 8

A CIP catalogue record for this book is
available from the British Library.

Typeset by Mac Style
Printed and bound in the UK by TJ Books Ltd,
Padstow, Cornwall.

MIX
Paper from
responsible sources
FSC
www.fsc.org   FSC® C013056

Pen & Sword Books Limited incorporates the imprints of Atlas,
Archaeology, Aviation, Discovery, Family History, Fiction, History,
Maritime, Military, Military Classics, Politics, Select, Transport,
True Crime, Air World, Frontline Publishing, Leo Cooper, Remember
When, Seaforth Publishing, The Praetorian Press, Wharncliffe
Local History, Wharncliffe Transport, Wharncliffe True Crime
and White Owl.

For a complete list of Pen & Sword titles please contact

PEN & SWORD BOOKS LIMITED
47 Church Street, Barnsley, South Yorkshire, S70 2AS, England
E-mail: enquiries@pen-and-sword.co.uk
Website: www.pen-and-sword.co.uk

Or

PEN AND SWORD BOOKS
1950 Lawrence Rd, Havertown, PA 19083, USA
E-mail: Uspen-and-sword@casematepublishers.com
Website: www.penandswordbooks.com

Contents

Acknowledgements

My thanks above all to my wife, Pam, who has often been a Watkin Widow during the years of my fascination with one of the great but unaccountably forgotten stars of the Victorian era. All authors have a touch of manic depression, the highs and lows as a brilliant chapter or phrase turns out the next morning to be fit only for the waste-paper bin. At such times – and when constructive criticism was needed or proofs had to be read – Pam has always been there to encourage me to go on writing the story of Edward Watkin – 'our man' as she calls him.

Most of my family and friends have been supportive, all have been tolerant, though eyes tend to roll when the Watkin word comes up in conversation yet again. One commented that Watkin seemed to pop up everywhere. He was right. That's what first interested me in this brilliant and prolific character.

Can I also record my thanks to Fergus Wilde, Librarian of the great Chetham's Library in Manchester for his encouragement and willingness to provide a home for the Watkin Collection. And to two members of the Watkin family: Fiona McNeil for her constant practical support and obvious pleasure in seeing the story of her great ancestor made more widely known and Richenda Goffin for her interest and for allowing me to quote extensively from her mother, Magdalen Goffin's fascinating book about Edward's father, Absalom. And a special mention to Sue Canterbury, the Curator of American Art at the Dallas Museum of Art in Texas, for her passionate interest in *The Icebergs*, the masterpiece that she calls the museum's *Mona Lisa*, which after a century when it had been 'lost' was found in the Watkin family home in Northenden, south Manchester and now hangs in pride of place in the DMA. I shall always be grateful to Mair Baulch, former matron, and to her late husband Gl[...] both of the Rose Hill Assessment Centre, for sharing their unique with me and for their friendship. It was Mair who discovered Church's lost masterpiece and started a fascinating trail that ended in Texas.

I want to thank all the holders of text and illustration copyrights for allowing me to use their material. My apologies to any copyright holders whom I have not been able to trace.

My thanks to everyone at Pen & Sword for their patience in answering my many questions in an unfailingly friendly and authoritative way. Special thanks to my editor, Alison Flowers, for her expert eagle eye.

My thanks to the committee of The Friends of Rose Hill and the former rector of St Wilfrid's Parish Church in Northenden, the Revd Greg Foster, for their early involvement in the Watkin story. This led to the formation of The Watkin Society. I want to record my appreciation of that Society's stimulating committee and especially to Jamie Rennie. I hope that if you enjoy *Victoria's Railway King* you may want to discover more about the amazing Edward Watkin through the Society's website at http://friendsofrosehill.org/the-watkin-society-watsoc.

Geoff Scargill
March 2021

List of Illustrations

Introduction

In 1874 the parish church of St Wilfrid's in Northenden, near Manchester, was being rebuilt. A subscription list was opened to meet the costs and Sir Edward Watkin, an MP and businessman living half a mile away, donated £500, the equivalent of £50,000 in today's money. That put him top of the public list, where he liked to be, so he was not best pleased when the local squire, Thomas William Tatton of Wythenshawe Hall, donated £850. Watkin made another donation, this time in his wife's name, of £350 – and ninepence.

That cheeky two-fingered ninepence was typical of Edward Watkin. He was a Victorian alpha male, who did not like losing and didn't mind making enemies. In fact, in his constant search for fresh omelettes, he quite enjoyed breaking eggs.

There were plenty of omelettes in the life of this remarkable man, who:

- was recommended to the Prime Minister as 'one of the cleverest men going'
- started a Channel tunnel in 1880
- built an Eiffel Tower that became Wembley Stadium
- helped create Canada
- built the last main railway line into London till High Speed 1
- helped bring down the price of bread – and a government
- created the biggest fishing port in the world – and a holiday resort next to it

In his lifetime spanning eighty-two years Edward Watkin – 'Nimble Ned' – the 'Railway King' – came tantalisingly close to being a great man. He was one of Victorian Britain's best-known characters. Yet today, he has been virtually forgotten.

Now his only surviving diaries have revealed someone far different from the dominant figure the public were familiar with. Like his father, Absalom, Edward Watkin suffered from self-doubt and depression. This is the story of the private as well as the public Edward Watkin – for the first time.

Chapter 1

Origins

Northenden, where Watkin lived most of his life and died in 1901, is a Manchester suburb on the River Mersey, 6 miles to the south of the city. That's it really. The high street, Palatine Road, is nothing special, two rows of nineteenth-century terraced houses, most of them converted into small shops and food outlets but not a patch on Manchester's famous Curry Mile just to the north. You wouldn't think there is anything to stop for here. But that's because the chances are that you have never heard of its greatest resident, Edward Watkin. And appearances can be deceptive. Northenden has a history.

When Watkin came to live here in 1834 it was a little Cheshire village, separated by the Mersey from its big energetic neighbour to the north, another world, unchanged in centuries. There was no bridge over the river at Palatine Road. There was no Palatine Road. The only ways in and out from the north were by a little ferryboat, a ford in dry weather or the bridge at Cheadle 4 miles away, built by Bonnie Prince Charlie's men as they rampaged their way south in 1745. Northenden was a rural oasis.

But Northenden's history stretches back far beyond Edward Watkin's family, in fact nearly 1,300 years. It gets a mention in the Domesday Book in 1068 but by then its first church was already 200 years old, one of only half a dozen in the whole of north-west England at the time.

When you turn off Palatine Road and walk by the river along Mill Lane then up Boat Lane and across Ford Lane – all names that conjure up Northenden's past – you come to the heart of old Northenden, where St Wilfrid's, the parish church that Edward Watkin helped to rebuild, still stands safe and solid on the highest ground for miles around. In 1951 those three lanes caught the attention of one of Britain's greatest architectural historians, Nikolaus Pevsner, when he published the first of his forty-six volumes of *The Buildings of England*, chronicling everything that took his eye throughout the country: 'The village was round the church above the ford and the mill. Narrow lanes, many pubs testify to this.' You're only a few hundred yards away from the fast-food shops here but there is still a rural feel. One building is Georgian and is called Northen House, the name Northenden went under for hundreds of years. Next to it is Cromwell Cottage, where the Roundheads stored their weapons in the Civil War before laying siege to the Royalists in nearby Wythenshawe Hall. In 1902 the butler in a local house killed his master and was then shot by the police. The men of Northenden wanted to drag the body down Boat Lane and throw it in the Mersey for Liverpool to sort out but the police came to the rescue and handed the remains over to the rector. Because of his crime the murderer could not be buried in consecrated ground, but the rector was a liberal. He buried the body behind the Victorian postbox in the wall of the churchyard. It is still there.

Three of the graves over near the back wall of the churchyard are grander than the rest. The middle grave is of Mary Watkin, Edward's first wife. On either side lie Edward and his father, Absalom, two men who during seventy years of the nineteenth century helped to change Manchester and Britain – in the son's case, four continents. In his lifetime Edward was dubbed the Railway King and for fifty years he strode the national and international stages. Possessed of amazing energy and brimming with daring schemes, he was known to his friends as Nimble Ned and a brilliant entrepreneur; to his enemies (he had plenty of those) as the Napoleon of the Railways and a fixer. At his death obituaries about him appeared in newspapers throughout the world.

If you follow an ancient path round the edge of the churchyard it's only a few hundred yards to what is left of Rose Hill House, where Absalom and Edward lived and died. By road it takes longer but if you drive through what everyone round here still calls 'the village' you'll come to Longley Lane. On a map of 1642 three long leas were important enough to have one of the local lanes named after them. Go down Longley Lane and you come to a side road full of potholes, more of a track now and a dead end. A few yards along, your way is barred by a fence and a padlocked gate, with the sand and cement of a builder's yard just beyond. A notice on the gate gives the address as 'Northenden Railway Station', a strange relic of history for the station has been closed now for over half a century and all its buildings have been demolished. Some contrast to 150 years ago when Northenden Station was neat and tidy with its own garden and a stationmaster like Bernard Cribbins in *The Railway Children*. In those days the chairman of the railway, Sir Edward Watkin, would alight there from his private carriage after one of his journeys from the European Continent or India or Africa or Canada or somewhere else a long way from sleepy little Northenden and his family home. It was half a mile from the station to the village, but it was conveniently close to the house of the chairman who built it. Watkin's brougham coach would need less than 5 minutes for the last stage of his journeys.

Opposite the old road to the station is a neat housing estate. The only way in from Longley Lane is a cul-de-sac called Bronington Close, but although the houses are all twentieth century, the entrance to the estate is flanked by massive old stone walls. These used to frame the enormous gates of the Watkin lands but all that is left of these is a single rusty hinge, hidden behind a tree. A couple of hundred yards along Bronington Close you come to a stretch of railings and the Sharstone, a huge boulder resting on a cast-iron stem and looking underneath its ivy like a giant mushroom. It was brought here by Sir Edward from one of his nearby farms, though one newspaper at the time reported that it was the tip of Snowdon in Wales. It is said to contain a time capsule. Behind it are the immaculate gardens of a large house built on higher ground and marked off from the rest of the estate not just by its railings but by electronic security gates. And its age. This is Ashley Grange, private luxury apartments. But the apartments and the name have only been here since 2003. For the previous 169 years of its existence this was Rose Hill House, the Watkin family home, where three prime ministers and the two great reforming statesmen of the mid-nineteenth century, Richard Cobden and John Bright, got out of their carriages after the short ride from Northenden Station, to be wined and dined by Sir Edward or his father. Those famous visitors and the two eminent Manchester men who lived and died in the house achieved for Rose Hill the status of a Grade II* listed building. The star puts it in the top 5 per cent of historic houses in England.

But there is no plaque on the railings to inform passers-by that this is a place of history. Only a plate fixed to an electricity substation near the gates tells us that this used to be Rose Hill, the home of the Watkins for eighty years, starting on a day in March 1834, when Absalom uprooted his family from their home in Higher Broughton near Salford and brought them to live in Northenden.

Chapter 2

Absalom Watkin – Semi-Detached Politician and Jealous Father

At the time of the move to Northenden the Watkin family was made up of Absalom, his wife, Elizabeth, their daughter, also called Elizabeth, and their three sons, Edward, John and Alfred. Edward was never close to his mother – she figures only rarely in his two surviving diaries. When she died, he wrote quite briskly: 'My mother died on Monday and we interred her remains on Friday so I ought to be at home.' When Absalom died, Edward wrote to a friend from Rose Hill: 'I have been summoned down here to attend the death-bed of my father, who cannot have many hours.' The handwriting is shaky, and the letter ends: 'I am in so much distress that you must excuse the incoherence of this note.' He commissioned a stained glass window in St Wilfrid's to his father's memory. There is no window commemorating his mother.

Edward's personal relationship with Absalom is the key to his development as an adult. This means that any study of the son's character and life needs to start with the character and life of his powerful father.

Edward grew up in a world dominated by his father's politics, which was the stage on which he played out his own public life. But his personal relationship to his father is key to understanding the most striking aspect of Edward's character: his need, amounting at times almost to a compulsion, to make his mark in the world, to be top dog. That ninepence in the public subscription list when St Wilfrid's Church was being restored is only one example in Edward's life of battles that sometimes seemed to have no other purpose except to be recognised, a characteristic that can be traced back to his father's enigmatic aloofness, which must have seemed to the young Edward to stem from a lack of affection towards him. He spent much of his life looking for a substitute.

Edward was born on 26 September 1819 (he and Queen Victoria shared the years of their births and of their deaths in 1901), when the Watkin family was living in Ravald Street, near what is now Manchester's Victoria Station, but just on the Salford side of the Irwell, where that river marks the boundary with its more famous neighbour. At the time Manchester was well on its way to becoming the first city of the Industrial Revolution, its blossoming wealth founded on cotton. Its nickname throughout the world was Cottonopolis. (The German for corduroy trousers is still 'Manchesterhose'.) Absalom was the owner of a thriving cotton warehouse in the best-regarded business part of town, High Street, and was a member of Manchester's growing and increasingly wealthy middle class. He was a family man and a Methodist local preacher, his name figured in lists of donors to worthy causes and he was so highly regarded in local society that he was invited to join Manchester's most prestigious club, the Literary and Philosophical Society, with a membership limited to sixty. He was a magistrate and died at Rose Hill at the age of 74 in December 1861.

But that summary of a seemingly conventional life hides the reality of a very different Absalom Watkin, a man who dedicated most of his adult life to a battle for reform that had as its epicentre Manchester. The more than 250 references to his public life in the archives of the *Manchester Guardian* and *The Times* provide the detail of his high reputation for fighting to improve the lives of the working classes in the city. Every initiative aimed at bettering the poorest in Manchester society mentions his name and his concern for reform went beyond Manchester. He championed the Society for the Promotion of National Education. (There was no national system of even primary education in Britain till 1870, nine years after his death.) With money and speeches, he supported the Poles and the Hungarians in their fight for freedom from Russian domination. He was a member of the Society for the Immediate Abolition of Slavery. In 1845 an advertisement appeared in the Manchester reform press for 'The Ladies Free-grown Cotton Movement'. It gave the names of the eleven businesses in the town that were refusing to sell cotton grown on slave plantations in America at a time when – contrary to what is nowadays believed – Britain's sympathies lay with the Confederate States. One of the eleven was Messrs A. Watkin and Son.

Absalom lived through a time when the tectonic plates were shifting throughout European politics, culminating in 1848, when governments and kingdoms fell. The political revolutions of the Continent of Europe largely passed Britain by. Instead, it became the birthplace of an Industrial Revolution that went on to transform Europe and the United States. But Britain's revolution did not involve just the invention of brilliant machines like the Spinning Jenny. It was a social revolution too, a time of unique social upheaval, as thousands of farm workers left their homes in the countryside to find work in the factories and mills of the towns of the north. The results were seen at their worst in the living and working conditions of the new working classes. Their houses formed squalid ghettoes built next to their belching, dirty workplaces. There were no planning regulations – the only requirement was that the houses should be cheap, with as many workers and their families packed into them as possible. The results were revolting. The farm workers had left their pigs in sties on their farms to come to Manchester, but the town had built new pig sties and the workers were the new pigs. A wonderful life for the few depended on the misery of the many, including children who were small enough to crawl under machinery to repair it and to climb inside chimneys. These were not human beings, creatures of grace. The usual name for workers in the factories and cotton mills in those days was 'hands'. Nothing was needed from them except their physical strength.

Absalom's concern for the poor was not typical of someone with his background. The classes virtually never met; they lived in parallel universes. In 1845, before his political career took off, the future prime minister, Benjamin Disraeli, wrote in his novel, *Sybil*:

> Two nations between whom there is no intercourse and no sympathy; who are ignorant of each other's habits, thoughts and feelings, as if they were dwellers in different zones or inhabitants of different planets; who are formed by different breeding, are fed by different food, are ordered by different manners, and are not governed by the same laws ... THE RICH AND THE POOR.

The well-meaning wealthy concentrated their efforts on what they called 'the deserving poor', the implication being that the rest had brought their wretched state on themselves. One writer told how he was asked by a woman with a bottle labelled 'Gin' in her hand: 'Is this the way to the workhouse?' 'No', he replied, pointing at the bottle: 'But that is.' According to a popular saying at the time, the quickest path out of Manchester was gin.

The French political thinker Alexis de Tocqueville described what he saw in Manchester in 1835:

On ground below the level of the river and overshadowed on every side by immense workshops, there stretches marshy land which the widely spaced muddy ditches can neither drain nor cleanse. Narrow, twisting roads lead down to it. They are lined with one-storey houses whose ill-fitting planks and broken windows show them up, even from a distance, as the last refuge a man might find between poverty and death. None-the-less, the wretched people reduced to living in them can still inspire jealousy in their fellow human beings. Below some of their miserable dwellings is a row of cellars to which a sunken corridor leads. Twelve to fifteen human beings are crowded pell-mell into each of these damp, repulsive holes. The foetid, muddy waters, stained with a thousand colours by the factories they pass, wander slowly round this refuge of poverty. Look up and you will see the huge palaces of industry. You will hear the noise of furnaces, the whistle of steam. These vast structures keep air and light out of the human habitations which they dominate; they envelop them in perpetual fog to the profit of one man. A sort of black smoke covers the city. The sun, seen through it, is a disc without rays.

It is a picture of Hell, with the dilemma of Manchester for liberals like Absalom set out starkly in de Tocqueville's final words: 'From this foul drain the greatest stream of human industry flows out to fertilise the whole world. From this filthy sewer pure gold flows. Here civilisation works its miracles, and civilised man is turned back into a savage.'

In 1844 the 25-year-old Edward Watkin was looking for material for a speech in support of a campaign to create public parks for the people of Manchester. He went to a part of the town that was completely unknown to him. His diary entry reads like an expedition to find the source of the Amazon:

On Monday we went on an exploration through the older part of Manchester near the Cathedral, along Millgate and up Shude Hill. Our object was to find cul-de-sacs and bad ventilation and easily we found them. Little tumbledown houses, broken windows, squalor, dung heaps before the doors. The people looking as if they had risen out of the dung to life, like maggots. As we passed into these blind courts the old hags and young watchers came to the doors to look out in wonder at the intruders. That within five minutes' walk of the Corn Exchange this should exist.

It was the same distance from Manchester Cathedral, but Shude Hill did not exist for the hundreds who worshipped there comfortably each Sunday.

This was Absalom's and Edward's Manchester. The town was Jekyll and Hyde, a marvellous place for the wealthy but a hellhole for the poor. The 1851 census for Angel Meadow, the beautiful name for what was by then Manchester's biggest slum, recorded that 18,347 people were 'living' in one square mile. The largest cotton mill was 8 storeys high and employed 1,500 people. (When Absalom moved his family the 6 miles to Northenden in 1834 the population of the village was 678.) In Manchester the average age of death in the working classes was 17 and even in the mid-nineteenth century 57 per cent of poor children in the town died before reaching their 5th birthday.

The working and living conditions of the mass of families in the centre of the town horrified Absalom. He was a devout Christian and it is a mark of the strength of his religious and political beliefs that in spite of his basically shy nature he fought through most of his adult life for the rights of working-class people in Manchester. Significantly, he chose politics as his vehicle for reform, rather than an often passive Church that saw suffering as inevitable or even desirable, an obstacle course ending in a better life in the hereafter.

Absalom's active role in politics began in 1815, when he became a founder member of The Manchester Men, a group of liberal politicians that went on to make the town's name for reform. His friends included national figures such as Richard Cobden and John Bright, John Edward Taylor (the founder and first editor of the *Manchester Guardian*) and Manchester's first MPs. He and a friend drew up the petition that publicised the Peterloo Massacre in 1819. He was one of the local leaders in the campaign that led to the Great Reform Act of 1832, which abolished the 'rotten' parliamentary seats that sometimes had only half a dozen electors. His greatest work was yet to come, however, for he was one of the leaders of the national campaign that was arguably the most successful reform movement in Britain's political history: the Anti-Corn

Law League. The Corn Laws (usually called 'The Bread Tax') had been passed in 1815 to protect English landowners from foreign competition by imposing tariffs on imported corn. The result was that the price of corn and therefore bread – the staple of the working-class diet – was kept artificially high. In years when the harvest was bad thousands starved to death. The League, organised from Newall's Buildings in the middle of Manchester, a few yards from Absalom's warehouse, was so successful that it brought down not only the price of bread but the government as well, split the Tory Party and led to the founding of the great nineteenth-century party of reform, the Liberals.

Absalom's leading role in the League has rarely been credited yet he was not only a founder member but was one of four men chosen by Cobden personally to draw up the aims of the Anti-Corn Law Association, which gave birth to the League. He was at the centre of the League's campaign, at first locally then nationally, as its vice-president. But his political commitment did not stop at abolishing the Corn Laws. He spent the best years of his life fighting for the rights of the poorest people in Manchester. He made speeches, served on all those committees and drew up the formal petitions to Parliament and the monarch, which were the only vehicle of protest at a time when Manchester had no MPs. (For many years his skilful petitions made him in effect the official voice of reform in Manchester.)

By 1849, when the repeal of the Corn Laws brought the campaign to its triumphant end and with the wind of reform filling his sails, Absalom could have gone on to represent the new, industrial heart of England as an MP, as did two of his friends. Yet this is where we come upon one of many surprises about Absalom Watkin. Apart from a quarrel in 1854 with his old friend, John Bright, over which side to support in the Crimean War (their correspondence appeared in newspapers in Britain, Russia and the United States and he wrote wistfully in his diary: 'All week I have been famous'), he chose virtually to vanish from public view. For someone who throughout his life had found it difficult to take decisions it was a momentous decision. Why did he take it?

The answer is that Absalom's political work had been at the expense of what he wanted for himself. Through all his years in the public eye he had been hating the dirt and the noise of industrial Manchester. He was secretly longing to 'get away from it all', to be on his own with his farm and his books.

Absalom's virtual retirement from public life at the end of the Corn Laws campaign must have come as a shock to his wider audiences, though there had been two straws in the wind hinting at the private man. In 1815 Archibald Prentice, his co-author of the petition protesting at the Peterloo Massacre, wrote to a friend: 'Mr Absalom Watkin, giving himself more to literature than to politic', and in 1834 he had exchanged life in teeming Manchester for the rural oasis of Northenden.

It was, however, not until the publication of Absalom's private diaries long after his death that the details behind the hints were revealed. It is a remarkable story in itself that we are able to read the diaries since in 1947, eighty-five years after Absalom died, the originals were destroyed. They had been in the possession of one of Absalom's great-grandsons, who in 1920 published *Absalom Watkin, Extracts from his journal 1814–1856*. It is a worthy volume but its limitations are shown in the word 'extracts' in the title and one significant sentence in its introduction: 'The extracts to be found in the following pages are here given as originally written, with the exception of those omissions which must usually be made when publishing, even to a limited circle, diaries which were originally intended for the eyes of their writer alone.' In other words, this version tells only part of the truth and presents only the public face of the man. It leaves out many of his private thoughts and actions, often the most interesting elements.

Seventy-three years later Magdalen Goffin, Absalom's great-great-granddaughter and an author in her own right, published *The Diaries of Absalom Watkin – A Manchester Man 1787–1861*. This very readable book is fleshed out with details that her staid relative did not want the general public to know and her own highly entertaining comments about her great-great-grandfather, affectionate but shrewd. By the end of the book, even though she does not make a final evaluation of Absalom – the biography is still to be written – you feel you know the man, warts and all – and there were plenty of those. Magdalen also lends a historical perspective to the Absalom Watkin story since she identifies him as a member of The Manchester Men.

The differences between the two editions of the diaries are referred to in Magdalen's introduction with a tantalising lack of detail:

In 1920 extracts from the diaries were edited by one of Absalom's great-grandsons and published by Fisher Unwin. The work was well done and accurate but, as the editor stated in his introduction, the entries selected included none of those passages 'originally intended for the eyes of the writer alone'. In other words, only Absalom's respectable, public face was revealed, the actual human being hidden. If matters had ended there, this book could never have been written. However, it happened that my father, E.I. Watkin, another of Absalom's great-grandsons, who as a child had lived with Sir Edward at Rose Hill and had a particular interest in the diaries, read the manuscript while he was an undergraduate at Oxford. Realizing how much the printed version had left out and fearing for the safety of the originals, he asked to borrow them and laboriously copied out by hand all that had been omitted. It was fortunate that he did so. In 1947, probably for snobbish reasons, the diaries were taken into the garden of Absalom's grandson, a former High Sheriff of Cheshire, and there were burnt.

'Fearing for the safety of the originals', 'probably for snobbish reasons', 'a former High Sheriff of Cheshire', 'there were burnt'. The tip of an intriguing family iceberg which sadly remains below sea level.

We owe a debt to Magdalen Goffin's father for suspecting – for reasons we can only guess at – that the survival of the diaries was under threat, and for his stamina in copying out the missing passages. What were called in the introduction to the 1920 version 'omissions' turn out to have amounted to over 200,000 words, more than two-thirds of Absalom's original manuscript. They include large sections which are in no way sensitive, but they flesh out the real Absalom Watkin. As a result, Magdalen Goffin's book is a valuable source of information about a man who would otherwise have been just a deodorised, bland public figure for us. And about his son. Magdalen's daughter, Richenda, has generously given permission for quotations from her mother's book to be included here.

Four extracts from his diaries capture the private Absalom Watkin, made more significant in that they span fifty years of his life. As a young man he went to stay with two friends in a cottage in High Legh, a farming village just to the south of Manchester. When he woke up the next morning, he watched a pair of swallows skimming about: 'Everything looked fresh with dew and glittering in the sun. These rural objects revived all my love of the country and made me desirous to live in such a place as this. Imagination was ready to tell me that here with my books and my garden every day would pass in peace and enjoyment.' Another passage was written just two days before he saw Rose Hill for the first time: 'I am made for moderation and a tranquil life. Splendour and a life of much publicity would only harass me.' The move to Northenden, only a short distance geographically, was for him an entry to another world:

> I listened to the noise of the wind among the trees, observed the distant lights, always brighter in windy weather, then noticed the gradual appearance of the stars and felt, as I had not felt for some time, the pleasure of living in the open air. Assuredly it is my duty to myself so to arrange my affairs as to pass much of my time out of doors and as free as possible from harassing cares.

Finally, at the age of 61, he wrote: 'Going to look for a volume I wanted, I was confronted by the sight of all my books. What an endless store of enjoyment and pleasure! While I keep them, I cannot be long unhappy.'

But in addition to letting us see the real Absalom Watkin, his diaries are fascinating documents for three more reasons. They are uniquely valuable for a study of Edward Watkin since they are virtually the only source of factual information about Edward's early years and reveal Absalom's strong opinions about his brilliant son. They also contain an insider's description of a period of social and political turmoil in Manchester, with Absalom and Edward Watkin as key players. Finally – and surprisingly – they reveal someone quite different from the serious-minded, often rather prim public Absalom Watkin.

As a young man he had planned to write a magnum opus but like many of his plans it remained a dream and he had to settle for describing people and incidents from his social life in his diaries. He had an eye for the quirky and a gift for a phrase. His descriptions of people he met at formal dinners are witty and not always gentle. Of one married couple, they 'scarcely opened their mouths except to put something into them'. Of another married couple: 'He, thin, pale and wanting some front teeth, apparently about fifty, with a look of insignificant amiability, saying little – she, perhaps thirty-five, plump, with dark eyes, a nose rather turned up, a very pretty mouth, complete self-possession and a rather graceful deportment.' He describes the wife, who is rather flirty, as 'taking little notice of her yoke fellow'.

Here is an affectionate description of his friend William Grime, who had a tendency to dramatise situations. (Many years earlier he had been bitten on the finger by his cat, which died the following day. Grime had been convinced that the cat had rabies and that he too would die.) It is midnight and there is a knock at Absalom's door. It is one of Grime's servants. His master is dying and has asked for Mr Watkin.

> I went. He was up, dressed and at prayer in the bedroom. He declared that he felt himself dying; requested me to lose no time in making his will. He sent the servant for his mother; his wife was extremely agitated and alarmed. I did not think him dying but thought it best to comply with his request. I sat down to write his will. As he dictated he drank freely of brandy and water; to 'keep him up', as he said. By degrees I ventured to tell him that I thought he was not dying. He persisted he was. His mother came. He took his leave of her. During this time he drank, as I learned afterwards, nearly half a bottle of brandy, mixed with warm water. This and his talking made him sweat most profusely, yet he persisted that he was cold and dying. I at length prevailed on him to get into bed. I sat by his side and made memorandums of what he wished me to do as one of his executors. At length he felt himself warm and began to think he should still live.

It was another twenty-four years before Grime died.

In the wider world of politics what the diaries reveal is that by withdrawing from public life at the end of the Corn Laws campaign in 1849 Absalom was finally making his choice between the demands of his public and private lives, a conflict that had been with him throughout his years of political campaigning. Sadly though, even if his decision gave him time to tend his farm and garden and read his books, two problems remained that still made him unhappy. Both must have had a serious effect on his son. The details are in the diaries.

The first was his chronic depression. Signs of illness had become apparent when he was 19 and working in Manchester for his uncle, 200 miles and several days' journey away from his family home in London. He had written a letter to his mother, Betty, in which he talked of committing suicide. His letter has not survived but his mother's reply has. 'Pray my dear son, what little strange extraordinary uneasynes [sic] has found the way to your breast? What plagues or crosses has rendered this motley lif [*sic*] of yours unhappy to make you think it's not worth living.'

Absalom shared his plagues and crosses with his private diaries and one poignant sentence written in 1827 captures his sense of isolation: 'I do not think or feel as the majority of mankind appear to do.' He writes about a visit to church:

> The bells were sounding tingle-tum, tingle-tum. It was a pleasing sight. The church was filled principally with the young and well-looking and cheerful countenances, good clothing, smart ribands and a profusion of evergreens and flowers gave to the whole thing a very animating and enlivening effect. I looked upon the assemblage attentively and with interest; I even noticed some of the most attractive so carefully as to retain a picture of them and their situation in church in my imagination. But when I had done this my thoughts passed to the future destiny of the individuals before me, to conditions of human mortality, and to the saddening reflection that all the animation and liveliness which I beheld must terminate in the silence of the tomb.

He saw the skull beneath the skin and it frightened him.

After a walk with his wife he writes: 'The evening was uncommonly beautiful, the moon brilliant, everything still, the leaves of the trees not moving, now and then the hum of a beetle and sometimes a distant noise of a coach on the road or of children shouting broke the silence. I felt all the beauty of the scene and was thankful.' It is a lovely tranquil scene and a fine example of Absalom's ability with words. What follows is all the more shocking: 'My heart continually reverted to sad and strange thoughts, and as I write this on my return, and while all the delicious softness of the place and the hour is strongly impressed upon my imagination, I feel deeply and hopelessly sad.'

Absalom's recurring bouts of depression must have been a prime cause of the panics and lack of purpose that are a feature of the diaries. Edward wrote of 'a want of direction and mind at the head of our family'. They also explain in part the emotional stone wall between him and his oldest son. He was prone to take solitary refuge in the fortress of his library, counting his books or checking the stock in his warehouse, seeking reassurance, like a child with its dummy or an anxious adult enjoying comfort food.

The second reason for Absalom's continuing unhappiness was his terrible relationship with his wife. As Edward grew up he had to watch the death of his parents' marriage.

For some years before the move to Northenden the diaries reveal Absalom's contempt for his wife. His dislike of Elizabeth was made worse by the state of his home. Rose Hill, like their first house in Broughton, was dirty and disorganised.

> I found at night that the cistern had been suffered to overflow into the necessary [i.e. the lavatory], notwithstanding my repeated cautions to Elizabeth on the subject. It is in this way that almost everything to which I wish her to attend is neglected. In the midst of extreme exertion on my part, I find in my wife only careless, sluttish, imprudent conflict.

Mrs Watkin (after the first few years of their marriage Absalom never refers to her in his diary as 'Elizabeth') took to drink and was often 'violent and intoxicated'.

Absalom's mother – always known as 'Betty' – had lived with the Watkins in Salford before they moved to Northenden. A week after her death in July 1830 Absalom decided to sleep in the bed in which Betty had died, 'to obviate any dislike which might be entertained to sleeping on the bed in which my mother died'. In the night he was woken by a 'disagreeable tingling and smarting'. When it was light he discovered that the bed and the curtains were swarming with bed bugs.

> I called my wife from her room and having made her witness the effects of her neglect, I destroyed more than twenty bugs on the pillow and on one side of the curtain and several on my nightshirt. I reflected that my mother, deprived of the use of her lower extremities and unable even to turn without assistance, had lain on the bed and on that bed had died.

A week later he had a bad night. The sheets were damp.

> I inquired what sheets I had slept in and if they had been aired. To my astonishment I found that the sheet on which I had slept was one of those from my mother's bed, the very sheet on which I had killed the bugs. It had lain in a heap since. I was enraged to the highest degree. I cursed the unfeeling hypocrite and was at last provoked to give her a box on the ear.

The gulf between Absalom and his wife was made worse by his flirting. He was a handsome man and his diaries show that he knew it. Like Wordsworth, he enjoyed recollecting in tranquillity his emotion about what were called in those days 'dalliances' by recording them in his diary, which he knew his wife would read. The diaries contain more than twenty entries about Mrs Stoneley alone, all appreciative. 'Mrs Stoneley was conspicuous in the dance, her tall and elegant figure being shown to great advantage by a dress of violet-coloured flowered crepe over white muslin.' Several are followed by passages in shorthand, which means that they were particularly private.

The diaries reveal in detail Absalom's changing relationship with his oldest son. When Edward was a child, it is clear that Absalom loved him. 'Gardened from a quarter before three in the afternoon till near seven o'clock. It was very hot and I kept close to my work, my little Edward helping me manfully.' In June 1827, when his son was 8, Absalom took his family out for the day to Beeston Castle, a beauty spot not far from Chester. They all climbed up to the castle and Absalom writes: 'I was particularly pleased with the enthusiastic ardour of my little Edward'. He goes on to make a prescient remark: 'If this boy is not spoiled by the folly of those about him, he will assuredly prove superior to the herd of mankind.'

On a visit to the countryside when Edward was 13 Absalom was moved by a feeling which sadly is usually missing from the diaries: an emotional bond between himself and another human being.

Walked with Edward. It was one of the most beautiful evenings I ever beheld. The sun was declining with mild radiance and gave at first a lustre, and then a richness, to every part of the landscape which his beams could reach, and after he had set, a glow to the western sky which heightened the beauty of everything. My mind was in unison with the scene. My little boy appeared to feel as I did. Edward and I gathered each a large handful of anemones as we went along. The bells of the church brought to the boy's mind Moore's song 'Sweet evening bells,' and he began to repeat it. The lines were in my thoughts at the same moment, and I was pleased to hear him. Full of these thoughts, I sat down on a lofty knoll, to which Edward had first climbed himself and then invited me, and looked at the trees, the flowers, and the sky, and listened to the birds and to the rush of the water and the music of the bells, and felt really happy and really thankful. We walked home observing the moon and the stars and the changes in the sky, and we talked of the universe and of its author, and I was happy.

The words 'my little boy appeared to feel as I did', 'the lines were in my thoughts at the same moment', 'invited me' and the simple ending 'I was happy' (something that Absalom so rarely feels) are the intimate feelings of a lonely man.

As Edward moved into his teens and began to develop a mind of his own, the earlier happy bonding with his father disappeared and the relationship between him and his father was shot through with strain. Some of Absalom's descriptions of his son could be written off as typical of the tensions inside a family when children are growing up. Even allowing for this, however, Absalom's epithets to describe the behaviour of his son during Edward's adolescence and as a young man are worthy of *Roget's Thesaurus*: rude, grossly insolent, lazy, rebellious, mad, base wretch, outrageous, brutal, unfeeling are only a selection. In his own diary Edward notes: 'My father and I do not hit it. [We] have had two or three flare-ups.' Absalom's diaries show there were more than two or three.

His problems with Edward stemmed from more than the spikiness of adolescence. He was dealing with a young man of exceptional ability and energy. His instinct was to try to rein him in and it was a mistake. A life of ordinariness was not going to be possible for the Railway King. Yet Absalom put him to work at the age of 14, along with his brothers, in the family warehouse. His plan was for Edward to become his partner and eventually to take over the business, which he re-named 'Absalom Watkin & Son'. We will see later what Edward thought of being condemned to what he dismissed as a 'life of calico'.

It is ironic that Absalom, who was spending so much time on politics, criticised his oldest son for neglecting the business for the same reason. Edward described his father as having 'no energy left for his own affairs'. Absalom was never a natural businessman. His Uncle John had said of the younger Absalom that he 'needed his face rubbing with a brick' and when he was looking back at the age of 65, Absalom wrote: 'It was necessary to work or starve, so I worked'. He rarely mentions his warehouse in the diaries.

By the time he was in his early twenties Edward had been captivated by the exciting world of the reform movement which his father had revealed to him. He had caught the political bug. In 1842 Absalom decided this had to stop. He planned to send his son to Italy in the hope that a break would cool his interest in politics. He wrote to his friend Richard Cobden to ask for his help in arranging a holiday abroad for Edward. (Since he had never been out of Britain he would have had no contacts in any other country.) Cobden was not fooled, as his reply shows: 'Am I correct in the supposition that you are actuated by a prudent desire to withdraw him for a season from the vortex of political excitement into which his ardour has plunged him?'

Absalom's hope was in vain. On Edward's return from Italy he continued where he had left off and pursued a career in politics that was to last in one form or another for the remaining fifty years of his life. The 'ardour' which Cobden saw in the 23-year-old Edward and which Absalom had written about after that family day out at Beeston Castle when his son was only 8 remained a characteristic of Edward until old age.

Absalom's attempts to channel his son away from politics were, however, not motivated only by a desire to see him carry on the family business. One feature of their relationship must have pained Edward particularly, since it stemmed from a less attractive streak in Absalom's character which runs through the diaries, sometimes as sulkiness but which in Edward's case often turned to jealousy at his son's achievements. The diaries provide plenty of evidence of Absalom's sourness towards Edward. He frequently snipes at his public speaking. He attended a testimonial dinner in London in honour of his son and commented: 'Edward did not speak very well.' There is another hint of waspishness in: 'Edward has had a very panegyrical vote of thanks from the directors.' His failure to give praise when his son would have wanted to celebrate his latest success must have been specially hurtful. These would have been the times when Edward was at his proudest and therefore most vulnerable.

In a Sherlock Holmes story *The Adventure of Silver Blaze*, a violent death occurs while a watchdog is on guard nearby. Holmes draws the attention of a Scotland Yard detective, Gregory, 'to the curious incident of the dog in the night-time'. Gregory says: 'The dog did nothing in the night-time.' Holmes replies: 'That was the curious incident.' The reason why the dog failed to bark was that it knew the criminal. The significance lay in what did <u>not</u> happen.

In Absalom's diaries there are many dogs that do not bark as far as Edward is concerned. When he was asked by Richard Cobden personally to organise a branch of the campaign to repeal the Corn Laws, he did so with such success that he quickly became its national chairman. His efforts are never referred to by his father. Nor is his part in the movement to establish public baths and washhouses for the poor in Manchester, a cause that would have been dear to Absalom's heart. In the early 1840s Saturday was a normal working day. On Saturday, 4 November 1843, however, most businesses in Manchester closed in the early afternoon. Absalom records the event in – for him – unusually clumsy language: 'Today, the giving of a half-holiday on Saturdays to people employed in warehouses, etc., was commenced.' He is avoiding identifying who had brought the change about – it was Edward and his friends. They had gone round the town persuading the most prominent employers to close their businesses at 2 o'clock. Absalom only mentions Saturday early closing once more, when he writes rather sniffily that it is hardly worth going in to work on a Saturday just for the morning.

In August 1844 Absalom attended a packed meeting in support of the campaign to open the first three public parks in Manchester and Salford, for which Edward was the secretary and main organiser. (As we shall see, Edward's work for this cause – he raised the equivalent of over a million pounds – was his lasting legacy to the two towns.) Absalom has room in his diary for: 'I was introduced by the Mayor to Lord Francis Egerton. I omitted to thank him for the pleasure, a great and enduring pleasure, which I have derived from his translation of Schiller's *Song of the Bell*'. I recollected this just after I left him and am still vexed.' He does not have room to mention Edward, who had organised the event and was the main speaker at it.

Absalom's omissions concerning the Athenaeum and the Trent Valley Railway are striking. Founded in 1835, the Athenaeum was the most prestigious cultural association in Manchester, with the grand aim of 'The Advancement and Diffusion of Knowledge'. (Richard Cobden said it was a 'manufactory for working up the raw intelligence of the town'.) By 1843, however, it was heavily in debt, mainly because of the cost of its magnificent new building in Mosley Street, now Manchester's Art Gallery.

(The architect was Sir Charles Barry Edward, the designer of the Houses of Parliament, who came at a price.) It was threatened with bankruptcy. Watkin, still only 24, was asked to join the board of directors with a brief to clear the Athenaeum's debts. He succeeded brilliantly by organising two enormous fundraising soirées, as public dinners were called at the time, in the Free Trade Hall. On the first of these glittering occasions Absalom's diary entry reads: 'Went tonight with my wife and daughter, Miss Wilson, John and Alfred to the Soirée of the members of the Athenaeum and their friends. It was held at the Free Trade Hall. Charles Dickens, the author of Nicholas Nickleby, was in the chair and the younger D'Israeli [*sic*], Milner Gibson etc were present.' For the second: 'The Annual Soirée of the Athenaeum at the Free Trade Hall. D'Israeli [*sic*] in the chair.' On neither occasion does Edward rate a mention.

Even more extraordinary are the diary entries referring to the new Trent Valley Railway Company in the Midlands. Edward had just been appointed as its secretary. Leaving his father's business marked a sea change in his relationship with Absalom. Perhaps that is why Absalom's diary is silent except for one terse sentence on 12 September 1845: 'Edward began his work at the "Trent Valley" office.'

The official opening of the new railway on 26 June 1847 gave Edward a chance to make his mark outside Manchester and he grasped it with both hands. It was a splendid occasion (described by Edward in his own diary as 'éclatante'), complete with 500 guests, including George Hudson, the first man to be called the Railway King, George Stephenson, and Prime Minister Sir Robert Peel, who performed the official ceremony with a silver spade, which Edward had the honour of carrying in a wheelbarrow. The guests sat down to lunch in a hall built for the occasion and were entertained by a military band. Absalom writes 400 words in his diary to describe the day and concludes: 'I enjoyed this day very much'. At no point does he make any reference to Edward, who had organised the whole triumphant day and arranged for his family to be guests of honour.

The cause of Absalom's jealousy is not hard to guess. In going to work for the new railway company Edward had burst out of the confines of his father's warehouse and Manchester. He was joining the most exciting industry of the day, his opportunity to step onto a larger stage, and make his name outside the world of cotton. Absalom's lack of confidence and dilemma about what he really wanted meant that he constantly dropped his gaze and backed off. The life revealed in his diaries is one of unresolved conflict: 'I will <u>try</u> to do my duty, but it is hard, very hard.' Edward was a complete contrast, at least in public. He took the world on, relished battles and usually won them. Perhaps Absalom saw in his son what he himself might have been and did not like his own reflection in the mirror.

Absalom's influences on his son were, however, not all negative. He was a fine speech maker, as was Edward. In November 1873, twelve years after Absalom's death, when his youngest son, Alfred, was being installed as Lord Mayor of what was by then the City of Manchester, one of Manchester's aldermen started the formal speeches by saying that he remembered 'old Absalom Watkin, who, years ago, was known as the most persuasive speaker who ever addressed a Manchester audience'. In addition to ability in public speaking, Absalom passed on to his son a flair for writing. Both men were asked in their early twenties to become newspaper editors and Edward contributed articles to the *Manchester Guardian* and the *Manchester Examiner*. Absalom's diaries, with their witty sketches of people that he met socially, led friends to urge him to become an author. Edward wrote six books, one of which, a description of his travels in the United States and Canada, sold out on the day it was published. Cobden wrote to Edward: 'You are far too modest in disclaiming literary pretensions. The artistic talent is in you if it were worth your while to take time to apply it.' Even though his cotton warehouse did not interest him, Absalom created and managed one of Manchester's most successful businesses, which did not cease trading until the 1960s. Edward's exceptional business skills were clearly inherited from his father. Although he was determined to leave the nest, he must have known that if he one day 'returned home' Absalom's business, along with a fine house and an extensive estate, would provide him with financial security.

But these positive influences on his son must be weighed against Edward's own depression, inherited from Absalom and recorded in detail in his own diaries, the apparent lack of affection from his father and the insecurity of his family life. If, as Wordsworth says: 'The Child is father of the Man', Absalom's lasting influence can be seen in the Railway King's need for a constant supply of fresh battles to prove himself. It was an itch that had to be scratched again and again during Edward's adult life.

In the end, though, of all Absalom's influences on his son, the most striking has to be Edward's enduring fascination with politics and by 1835 he was about to take up this portion of his inheritance. It was the start of Edward Watkin's Manchester Years.

Chapter 3

Changing the Face of Manchester

On 15 September 1830, perhaps with a sense of history about to be made, Absalom took his family to see the first timetabled passenger train in the world arrive in Manchester from Liverpool. He was now 43 years old and his son, Edward, was a few days away from his 11th birthday. By the time Edward was 43 he was becoming famous – not just in Britain – as a Railway King.

The first step in Edward Watkin's public life was in the summer of 1835, when he was 16 years old. It was a small step but seen in the context of his father's life and what was to follow, it was a significant one simply because it was political. He acted as a 'check clerk' at a parliamentary by-election, making sure that voters had done their duty. Three years later marked the start of his Manchester Years, ushering in a decade which featured a succession of remarkable public achievements by a young man who was not even 30 by the time it ended. By then, however, he was working in Britain's dynamic new industry, the railways, and had turned his back on Manchester and his father's warehouse.

We know from his diaries how Edward felt about his brilliant public successes during that special decade. They also give us a unique insight into his feelings about his marriage and the birth of his son.

Like his father, Edward kept diaries throughout most of his life. At his death these passed to his son and when Sir Alfred Watkin died in 1914 they remained in the possession of his wife, Lady Catherine Watkin, for a further thirty years. Just before her death in 1944 at the age of 90 she continued a family tradition started six years earlier with Absalom's diaries. She burned them.

Why? The reasons may well have been in part personal. Watkin was notoriously outspoken in his public views so what he wrote in private would certainly have contained material that was embarrassing or even offensive to a lady in her nineties, whose father had been a senior priest of the Anglican Church in Canterbury. Furthermore, some of the indiscretions may have referred to the relationship between Sir Alfred and his wife. Their marriage had been childless and seems to have been unhappy. Alfred resided for long periods at the railway hotel at Charing Cross Station. He kept a number of mistresses there, who were known by the staff of the hotel as the 'ladies in waiting'. Perhaps burning her father-in-law's diaries was the only way to retain control of them for someone who had had the power of possession for thirty years and was approaching the end of her life. After all she had nobody close to leave them to. Perhaps she even saw destroying the diaries as a last act against a husband whom she had not loved.

There might, however, have been another, less personal reason for getting rid of the diaries. By 1944, in the middle of a world war, Edward Watkin had been largely forgotten as a public figure (forty-three years had passed since his death and it would be another sixty years before the first biography would appear). Lady Catherine perhaps decided it was time – literally – to turn the page on her father-in-law since he was no longer of any interest to the world.

Somehow, two small notebooks became separated from the rest. Watkin's great-granddaughter, Miss Dorothea Worsley-Taylor, found them in papers that had belonged to her grandmother, Watkin's daughter, Harriette. They are now in The Watkin Collection of the Chetham's Library in Manchester. What makes them specially valuable is that they cover one of the most significant periods in the life of the man who became a Railway King.

The years when Watkin's sap was rising coincided with an explosion of municipal energy in Manchester. As the birthplace of the Free Trade movement, which would establish Britain as the dominant world power of the nineteenth century, it had been transformed from a small market town with a population at the start of the eighteenth century of fewer than 10,000. When Absalom arrived there in 1801 Manchester had been still quite rural. An advertisement appeared in the local press that year for the sale of a 'windmill, with dwelling house, and extensive grounds, with a pond in the centre'. Where the windmill used to be is now Manchester's great Town Hall and 200yd away is Windmill Street. Thirty-seven years later Absalom sat in a friend's office in the middle of Manchester and noted that it was 'strongly scented by the perfume of the goats from the stable beneath'. By the mid-nineteenth century Manchester's population was increasing at the rate of 50,000 a year and had already reached 300,000, with hundreds of factories and teeming streets. And some of its inhabitants at least were determined to do something about the appalling living and working conditions of the many.

The national Anti-Corn Law League was being organised from Newall's Buildings in Market Street, just round the corner from Absalom Watkin & Son's warehouse. What a setting Manchester was for a young man like Edward, bursting with energy and radical zeal. Every morning must have seemed like the first day of spring, and life at Rose Hill must have been specially heady stuff for him, listening to great men arguing and plotting, often staying overnight then chatting at the breakfast table while he was listening. He longed to be part of this brave new world. One evening in 1837, when Edward was 18, Absalom was invited to dine at Richard Cobden's house in Quay Street in Manchester. Edward wanted to go to what promised to be a political evening to savour but his father made him stay at home. There was a scene, but Absalom went without him.

However, recognition of his talents soon followed and at a high level. Cobden's numerous visits to Rose Hill had provided him with plenty of opportunities to observe the young man and he wrote to Absalom about Edward, 'for whose character, talents and energy I have a great respect'. Edward must have noticed and been flattered by the great man's approval of him, even more so when in 1838 Cobden personally chose him for a special role in the Anti-Corn Law League. Worried that the League was becoming dominated by the middle classes, he asked Edward to set up an offshoot in Manchester among the local operatives, in other words the factory and cotton mill workers, and early in 1839 the Operatives' Anti-Corn Law Association of Manchester was formed. Edward was its secretary and immediately showed his flair for organisation by dividing the town into branches, each with its own officers. Soon there were Operatives' Associations in Leicester, Leeds and Huddersfield and within two years the Association had branches throughout the country, all organised by Edward from Manchester. Watkin, still only 21, was elected national chairman and began to set up regional conferences and address workplace meetings. On 13 January 1840 Absalom went to a League dinner in Manchester in a pavilion on the site where the Free Trade Hall was later built. The tickets cost 10*s*. (50p) and 3,000 were purchased. On the following evening Edward organised a dinner for the Operatives'

Association in the same pavilion. Tickets were 1s. (5p) a head and 5,000 sat down to the meal.

In 1841 the Operatives' Association published its own newspaper, the *Anti-Monopolist*. (Among the campaigners, 'monopolist' was a term of abuse for landowners, who could sell their corn at exorbitant prices because they were protected by the Corn Laws.) Watkin had the first six issues bound and placed in his private library. They are now in the Chetham's Library in Manchester, the only copies to have survived. They give a unique insight into an organisation which Watkin was running on Cobden's behalf.

The aims of the new Association are set out in the first issue. They include 'the dethronement of lordly idleness and the union of the masses'. The issue pokes fun at a speech given to the conservatives of Rutland by their future Tory MP:

> Ladies and Gentlemen – I must bring in the ladies for I see there are some pretty blue bonnets. It's a very fine day. Everything seems to favour us: it's a very fine day; there is a good number of flags and a very good band: it's a very fine day for the corn. I am a conservative. I have come forward as a candidate for Rutland at the request of several gentlemen: it's a very fine day. I hope our cause will be prosperous. I will not detain you any longer; it's a very fine day.

The newspaper contains several reports on meetings where Watkin took the chair, made the keynote speech or proposed motions. In one speech at what is described as 'a conference of the working classes', he is reported as saying: 'The people are entitled to receive compensation from the aristocracy, who have fattened themselves from their sufferings.' He was becoming a prolific writer of letters to the press, often sent from 26 High Street, Manchester, his father's warehouse. Cobden wrote him a personal letter of encouragement: 'You and your little band are doing wonders by keeping alive the Anti-Corn Law agitation.'

In the year he organised the dinner for the operatives in Manchester, Edward made his first political speech in public, opposing the Corn Laws. It annoyed the local vicar, who was a Tory. He also wrote an open letter to Prime Minister Robert Peel, again on the Corn Laws. Criticising the prime minister shows a remarkable amount of self-confidence for a 21-year-old and the letter drew rare praise from his father, who wrote in his diary: 'It does great credit to Edward's industry and argumentative powers.' That is the only time Absalom refers in his diary to Edward's involvement in the Anti-Corn Law campaign, though it must have been a frequent topic of conversation in the family at the time.

In August 1842 an article in *The (London) Times* reported on 'The State of the Manufacturing Districts'. From the standpoint of the authorities it was not good. The correspondent reported the formation of a new 'Manchester Complete Suffrage Union'. Its aims included votes for all men above the age of 21, constituencies of equal size, payment for all MPs and secret ballots. The Executive Committee, according to *The Times*, contained 'Chartist Agitators, Anti-Corn Law Agitators, Socialists and authors of several seditious placards recently pasted upon the walls of Manchester.' One of the Executive members listed is Edward Watkin.

In 1843 Edward led a campaign for Saturday half-day closing in Manchester's businesses. Until then, Saturday had been an ordinary working day with only the Sabbath available for rest and recuperation – and church, though contrary to what is generally believed, most working class men spent their Sundays in Victorian times in the ale-house or enjoyed with their wives once-a-week privacy after they had sent their children off to Sunday School. Simply by knocking on doors Watkin and a group of his friends persuaded 500 employers in Manchester to close their doors at 2pm on Saturdays. At the time Watkin wrote: 'The new regulation bids fair to be the fruitful parent of happiness to the vast number of sensible people and at no harm to the fools.' He explained that last phrase in a speech he made to the Manchester Arts Club some years later: 'It was done without any Act of Parliament. [We] simply set to work and agitated and repudiated the suggestion put forward by some of the starched and stiff old merchants who went to chapel that the employees, if they got the half-holiday, would spend their time in debauchery and folly.' The reference to Parliament is to underline that it was another seven years before the rest of the country caught up with Manchester and it had to pass an Act of Parliament first.

The Saturday 'half-day holiday', as it was called, is just one example of what Mancunians used to say at the time: 'What Manchester does today, the rest of the world does tomorrow.'

In the same year – 1843 – Watkin rescued the Manchester Athenaeum from bankruptcy. He had been gaining a local reputation for energy and organisation through his work in the Anti-Corn Laws campaign and the invitation to become a director of the Athenaeum was basically so that he could join a fundraising committee to try to clear the debts. He offered to organise two public dinners, soirées, in 1843 and 1844 – and persuaded a committee of hard-headed Manchester businessmen to back him. What marked his plans out was the enormous number of tickets he sold. The Unique Selling Point was his invitation to two super-stars of the day to be the after-dinner speakers. The first was Charles Dickens, the sensational author of *The Pickwick Papers, Oliver Twist* and *Nicholas Nickleby*, fresh from a triumphant speaking tour of America and at the height of his literary powers. (It was while he was in Manchester for Watkin's 1843 soirée that the idea of *A Christmas Carol* flashed into his mind in what he called 'a great gust of creative imagination'.) The other was Benjamin Disraeli, a successful novelist who had been born a Jew but whose father had had him baptised into the Church of England as a poke in the eye for the local synagogue when he fell out with the members. In 1843 Disraeli had been an MP for only seven years and was just starting a political career that was to see him become Chancellor of the Exchequer and prime minister and Queen Victoria's favourite. He was, however, already the leader of the 'Young England' movement of romantic Tories with ideas born on the playing fields of Eton and Cambridge (neither of which Disraeli attended). He could not have been further away politically from Edward Watkin. In particular, he was a supporter of the Corn Laws and in 1843 those laws were what Manchester, Absalom and Edward hated most. But Disraeli was a sensation wherever he went and even men who despised him politically wanted to see him in the flesh, as did their wives. It is typical of Edward's pragmatic approach to life that while he was concentrating on raising money he was not bothered about Disraeli's politics. It was that same pragmatism that would in the end set the limits to his political career.

The way he persuaded Disraeli to take part in both soirées revealed a degree of flair bordering on chutzpah. On the day before the first of the soirées was held Richard Cobden wrote to tell Watkin that Disraeli was in town, staying at a hotel near the Watkin warehouse. Although Cobden was no fan of Disraeli and his supporters ('sad political humbugs'), he said 'Ben' would make a good chairman for the Dickens soirée the following evening. Edward must have been up to his eyes in last-minute arrangements but he recognised an opportunity, dropped everything and went to the hotel.

> Mr. Disraeli was out, but I found Mrs. Disraeli at home. She was a little, plain, vivacious woman; one who, like an india-rubber toy, you have only to touch, and it issues sound. But she was obviously no common-place woman. Her comments upon what she had seen already in Manchester were acute, and, at times, decidedly humorous. They were those of a shrewd observer. We became good friends. She promised, both for herself and her husband, to attend the soirée; and, in answer to my further request that Mr. Disraeli would speak, she replied: 'Benjamin will speak. He can always speak at ten minutes' notice.' The soirée was brilliant. Dickens was at his very best; and it must have been difficult indeed to follow so admirable a speaker. But Mr. Disraeli certainly shared the honours and the applause of this great meeting.

The incident is pure Edward Watkin. He had never met Disraeli before yet he had the nerve not only to call uninvited on an up-and-coming politician but when he found Disraeli was not there he was able to sweet-talk Mrs Disraeli into agreeing that her husband, who was known to have a giant ego, would appear, even though he would not have top billing.

The evening was such a success that Watkin invited Disraeli to be the main speaker the following year. Cobden was not happy with that decision, but Watkin knew his audience. The second soirée, in 1844, was another sensation. Disraeli delighted his audience with a witty speech and at the end Cobden, ever the gentleman, led three cheers for Mrs Disraeli. According to the report in the *Manchester Guardian*, Disraeli caught the mood by responding that:

> Only one circumstance could gratify Mrs Disraeli more and that was that they should clear the hall as soon as possible and commence dancing. (Laughter) It being now eleven o'clock, the floor of the hall was soon cleared of seats; and the dancing commenced with great spirit and continued with unabated vigour to an early hour in the morning.

The report ended: 'We have omitted to state that at least three thousand two hundred persons were present at this soirée – the most extensive and brilliant entertainment ever given by the Athenaeum.' Edward echoed this when he wrote in his diary: 'Everything brilliant, fine, grand, effective. I feel astonished at our success. It convinces me that I have a forte in getting up and organising … meetings. I have had all sorts of congratulations etc today, and certainly the meeting will have a great and most useful effect in the country.'

The two evenings raised the equivalent of £200,000 towards clearing the Athenaeum's debt and made Watkin's reputation, and not only locally, for the *Manchester Guardian* carried a further report a week later in which it wrote that the evening had 'aroused interest not only in this country but on the Continent'.

After a private dinner in Swinton near Manchester Watkin wrote a description of Disraeli:

> We had a very pleasant evening. Disraeli threw off all restraint – told us some spicy stories, some very silly. His manner is elegant and to my mind intensely yet quietly affected. His face is a singular one – a little Jewish – eyes fine, dark and languishing, a clear pale face and at times destitute of all recognisable expression. His face is one of those which make you doubt. He has the art of concealing what he feels and you look in vain to his face for anything which can prove to you that he is influenced in reality by what you say to him. His morality – in minor matters at least – is lax. All this made me set him down as an artful but clever dodger. Cooke and Taylor, however, say there is more heart and good nature about Ben than people think but that he is eaten up by vanity.

That vignette has more than a touch of his father's style.

In 1844 Watkin started to raise money for what would be his greatest legacy to the citizens of Manchester and Salford: the first public parks in both towns. The first reference in his diary is on 30 March 1844: 'I have commenced endeavouring to obtain a public walk or ground in the suburbs of Manchester.' (Initially Watkin always refers to parks as 'walks'. One of the Victorians' favourite pastimes on Sundays became promenading in their best dress and being seen.)

Manchester had been slow to see the need to provide breathing space and recreation for all its citizens but in particular the poor. Birkenhead on the Wirral had led the way with the world's first public park in

1843. (When New York was planning its Grand Central Park in 1858 a delegation was sent to Birkenhead to see how it was done.) In June 1844 a leader in the *Manchester Guardian* said: 'Manchester stands forth in the notoriety of being almost the only town of importance in the kingdom entirely destitute of parks, promenades, or playgrounds of any kind, for the free use of its population. It offers its toiling inhabitants nothing better than the dirt and dust of streets and highways.' That leader was one of a series of articles campaigning for public parks. Watkin provided most of the facts and the arguments.

On 16 April his entry reads: 'Busy with a requisition to the Mayor to call a public meeting about public walks – also seeing people and writing for *The (Manchester) Times* and *The Guardian* on the subject. I think we shall work it.' On 12 May he writes: 'During the week I have been very busy with the Public Walk requisition. I presented this on Friday to the Mayor, who is to call a preliminary meeting.' On 18 May: 'I have during the week written a little pamphlet on public walks, which is published today.' The pamphlet was called: *A Plea for Public Walks*, and on 25 May he writes: 'The "*Plea for Public Walks*" has appeared by example in *The Guardian* twice.'

In August 1844, at a meeting with the Mayor of Manchester, Watkin was appointed as one of two secretaries to a new Committee on Public Parks and by 11 September the campaign had taken off. The *Guardian* carried a report on a 'Great meeting of the working classes, last evening.' It was held in the new Free Trade Hall, with nearly 6,000 men present and 'a goodly number of ladies in the gallery'. Watkin made the keynote speech: 'What we want is to let more daylight into our towns; to give Manchester more health-giving lungs. It is a disgrace to Manchester that it has been so long without such places. It is said that the working classes would not use these places if they had them. Our reply is: "Just give them the opportunity".' (Applause.)

Watkin said that he and the other secretary had already started canvassing for money to buy land (in his diary he calls it 'cadging'). Never a shrinking violet, he wrote to Prime Minister Robert Peel to ask for a donation, and in April 1845 he went to 10 Downing Street as part of a deputation seeking government support for parks in Manchester and Salford. (A few days before, he had been asked to 'draw up a case for our guidance'.)

We mustered in a sort of Library at Downing Street and when ready were shown into a large room where Peel sat behind a table with a desk surrounded by books and papers. When we entered he rose and requested us to be seated. We opened our case – had a talk of 40 minutes. I spoke three or four times and got £3000 offered! We wanted £80000!! So much for our first rebuff.

Peel did, however, donate £1,000 of his own money.

The numerous diary entries over the next few months show just how much effort Watkin put into establishing public parks. He led the campaign. The entry for 20 May 1845 reads: 'During last week I bought for the Public Parks Committee Lady Houghton's land.' (This became Manchester's first public park, Philips Park, named after his fellow campaigner, Mark Philips, Manchester's first MP.) But the campaign exhausted him. 'I wish my public Parking was over. It won't do Edward at all. Gird up thy loins for the fight with thyself which must be waged.'

The campaign for public parks in Manchester raised nearly £19,000, which equates to well over £1 million today. Most of the local wealthy families, such as the Moseleys, the Wiltons, the Ducies and the Stamfords, are missing from the published lists of subscribers. But the working classes of the town made 537 donations of 5s., 481 of 1s. and 173 of sixpence. At the end of the campaign Watkin bought three parcels of land and on 5 August 1845 he and the other secretary of the campaign handed over the deeds to the Manchester and Salford councils. They were received with prolonged applause and given silver tea-sets at a special meeting of Manchester Council. The Town Clerk said: 'These are the names which are to be handed down in connection with the Manchester public parks to all posterity.'

A flavour of the radical spirit of Manchester at the time can be seen in a warning by Archibald Prentice, who with Absalom Watkin had drawn up the petition against the Peterloo Massacre in 1819, that Manchester must make sure that 'aristocratic robberies of public rights' did not result in the lanes leading to the new parks being deliberately blocked.

On 22 August 1846 (four days after the birth of Edward's son, Alfred) Philips Park and Queen's Park in Manchester and Peel Park in Salford (named after Robert Peel) were opened to the public. The report in the *Manchester Guardian* began: 'Saturday was a memorable day in the annals of Manchester'. It spread over three pages. There were thirty-two carriages and twelve coaches in the processions to the three parks, a sign in Victorian times of the importance of the occasion. The *Guardian* emphasised that the absence of royalty and other 'notable' people meant that 'one great fact' was clear: 'The dedication of these three noble parks to the people for their use and recreation for ever was presented alone to the contemplation of the community.'

The *Guardian* commented later that on the Sunday following the opening of the parks the number of people appearing before the courts as drunk and disorderly in their areas had halved.

The entry in Watkin's diary for the day shows just what the day meant to him personally:

> On Saturday we celebrated the opening of the Public Parks to the people. Although I desired to absent myself, Polly [this was his pet name for his wife, Mary] would hear of nothing but my going as she said it would be 'something to tell our son and for our children to be proud of'. I therefore went and was 'celebrating' from 10 in the morning to 10 at night. We had a glorious day in every way – fine weather – good procession – plenty of people and a fine spirit of enthusiasm. It was really cheering to see the people happy and rushing in in one never ending long stream on the opening of the gates. I felt proud at those moments and felt that I had <u>done something</u> for once.

The underlining is Watkin's.

The three parks are monuments to Watkin's vision, persistence and outstanding organisational skills. They are also an early sign of his ability – he was only 26 – to persuade people to part with their money, something that would establish Nimble Ned's reputation during the next fifty years.

After his rescue of the Athenaeum and his leadership of the parks campaign Watkin was now being talked about, not just in Manchester, as a young man of extraordinary confidence and flair – and with the ability to deliver. But the contrast between the pleasurable successes of public life on the one hand and his private life in Rose Hill and in his father's cotton warehouse on the other was becoming acute, as his diaries record.

In the 1840s – as in the rest of his life – the public Watkin seemed to be bursting with self-confidence. He was to become the pugnacious leader, the Napoleon, of Britain's railway industry. The private man was a workaholic who from his twenties onwards suffered from anxiety, depression and nervous breakdown. The two surviving diaries describe in detail the anguish that the increasingly brilliant public figure was privately going through.

Just how vulnerable the Railway King really was is shown most vividly in what he writes about his family's troubles. His brother John suffered a nervous breakdown while at university and it was Edward, not Absalom, who travelled to Oxford to comfort him and bring him home to recover. His sister, Elizabeth, suffered for many years from a painful nervous complaint. Edward's diary contains several entries that show how his sister's illness distressed him. The entry for 13 January 1845 reads: 'Thursday evening at home trying to make my sister (who was distracted with Tic douloureux) a little better.' Three days later he writes: 'My sister is still exceedingly ill. I don't know what we should do. It is really miserable to see her in this state without having the power of alleviating her suffering.'

The pressures of his family meant that Edward was often in despair:

Heaven help me. Sister ill, Father ill. John perpetually depressed. Alfred not well and discontented, mother old and myself weak enough and imbecile enough.... I can truly say that I am myself alone. I have to do all for myself surrounded with many hindrances and with much that weakens and wounds the spirit. I am not respected at home and am considered, I imagine, too much as the family drudge who has no right to do anything but slave for the rest.... I fear that to sell calicos will be the highest office I shall fulfil in this life.

Worries about his own health dominate the diaries:

From the 1st Jan to April 15 I was extremely and at times overwhelmingly occupied. I worked, at times, nearly night and day and over and over again desecrated the Sabbath with continuous business. From the 15th of April till at last August my life was one piece of suffering – at times of horror. Positive suffering – intolerable weakness – the fear of all sorts of disorders – the horror of a sudden death – all daily and nightly.

He describes 'loss of thought and sense of suffocation'. Problems with his bowels are a recurring theme. At one point he writes: 'My damn bowels again. I wish I had none!!!' At another: 'I must ... conquer this absurd … dependence on nerves, bowels, east winds and rain. It won't do Edward at all. Those everlasting disorders of the bowels … are the only "hereditaments" I ever perhaps shall inherit from my ancestors.'

Like his father, he dreads speaking in public: 'At both meetings I spoke tho' I was dreadfully nervous.'

There is, however, a positive side to this picture of seemingly unbearable pressure. The strain that he is working under is a stimulant. 'My work just now takes me about a good deal and I encourage locomotion as I think the moving about does me good.… I have little doubt that the perpetual hurrying about and change of scene and air has been of service to my nerves and to my health generally.' In later life Watkin wrote: 'The best work and the most reliable is done under conditions of high tension and nervous strain.' This reinforces an earlier comment that his poor relations with his father may have spurred him on to higher things.

The only reference to relaxation from the pressures of his work recalls his father's pleasure at being away from the pressures of a town. 'So soon as I get a week or two at the sea-side I shall rally quite. This is really a source of gratification.… Away to see the castle which pleased me very much. The pleasure which beautiful scenery and ruins always have upon me quite restored me.' On another occasion when he has been away on railway business he takes 'the opportunity of visiting a fine old church' and chatting with the vicar.

He is often elated, sometimes extremely so: 'Well, must try the impossible of the moment. What a beautiful condition I am in! … Nothing, no difficulty is too strong for the power I have at my disposal.… I have again felt a consciousness of power, an inborn strength. I can hardly stop laughing at myself.' His mood swings are almost bipolar: 'On Tuesday excited with work … there was no sorrow or trouble. The day after I thought differently – the day after and today hard at it again – I feel my feet once more. What a weathercock.… Last night … a brilliant spectacle. This morning dull and spiritless.' (One of the cruellest effects of depression is to go to bed feeling well and to wake up the next morning feeling flat. On the moors above Stonyhurst College in north Lancashire is a memorial stone, asking for prayers for the soul of James Well, who died on 12 February 1834. It ends: 'Oft evenings glad, Wake mornings sad.')

His feelings about himself sometimes amount to loathing: 'I shall soon be despised by others as much as I despise myself'. He describes 'quailing at my own horrid self'. This sense of revulsion perhaps originates in an emphasis – not unusual in Victorian society – on guilt, often expressed in religious terms: 'While ill I resolved over and over again to eschew wickedness and worldliness and to strive after godliness – I meant it – and tried to do it.… I blush to say that my moral condition is not improved.… Intellectually speaking I look back with shame at no improvements.'

In the summer of 1844, however, Watkin's private life took a turn for the better. In the July he and his father were guests at a wedding in Oldham. The bride was one of the daughters of Jonathon Mellor, a respected local businessman, a magistrate and a supporter of the Free Trade movement. It was a significant day, as he records in his diary three days later: 'The two eldest girls were intelligent and one, Mary BriggsX, pretty and interesting'. (The letter X, used in a more decorous age to indicate something sensitive, is a sign that his feelings had been stirred.) A few lines later he writes: 'X has been running in my head a good deal since Wednesday – fine girl.' On 14 August he writes about a social occasion where he meets Mary again: 'Miss Mary Mellor, who became my precious [i.e. 'darling'], and I kept one another company. A nice girl. I feel rather fond of her.' She is a 'warm-hearted, frank girl – and heart is what I want.' In spite of her 'want of neatness and a vulgarity of ideas', he feels 'very amorous'. He wonders whether to write to Mary's father to ask his permission 'to pay my addresses' and with an echo of his father: 'I fear to take any step yet fear not to take one.'

Then comes a judgement which would be borne out in their life together: 'I think she will be a good manager.' The contrast with his mother is obvious and may have been in his mind as he wrote. He had seen many examples of how Absalom's wife could not 'manage' Rose Hill. The contrast must have been painful for his father too for Mary would go on to provide the stability in Edward's life which Absalom lacked.

However, being in love makes his situation worse in one respect. He despairs over his lack of money and a settled career: 'I want to marry. I am keeping a woman I love indefinitely waiting and I cannot tell when or how I must manage to furnish my house or keep my wife and myself after I am married!' Mary came from a wealthy family.

In the summer of 1845, the sun began to shine in Watkin's world. He was 'headhunted' by the Trent Valley, Midlands and Grand Junction Railway, who were looking for a secretary to organise their new company. On the morning of 30 August he met the directors. His diary entry reads: 'At half past one had the appointment offered. To cut the matter short I have undertaken it and shall begin in a fortnight.' The way ahead was now clear and two days later he writes in his diary: 'On Wednesday next I shall be married. I have everything in apple pie order and hope to be happy.' From 30 August to 24 September the diary is blank and the only description of the marriage day is a rather curt entry in his father's diary on 3 September: 'To Oldham, a continuous ascent of nearly four miles. There Edward and Mary Mellor were married.' On 24 September Edward's own entry reads: 'My marriage ... took place in good fine weather and under all sorts of favourable circumstances on Wednesday morning Sep 3.'

After the wedding breakfast Edward and Mary honeymooned in Chester for a week and went to live in their new home in Failsworth, near Oldham. He took up his new post immediately on his return. Two weeks later was his 26th birthday. Life must have seemed like the songwriter's bowl of cherries, there to be dipped into.

Typical, however, of Watkin's chronic tendency to worry, his new family responsibilities frightened him and increased his sense of guilt, particularly after the birth of his son in August 1846.

> A new duty – that of a father – now rests upon me – and both regard for the souls of my wife and child should drive me to amendment. – day after day and year after year of opportunity neglected and blessings ungratefully received – alas what folly and gross delusion! 'What shall it profit a man if he gain the whole world and lose his soul' [This is a quotation from St Mark's Gospel. Edward chose the same words for a memorial he erected in his father's memory in front of Rose Hill House] – and how horrible what a hell-pain would arise from the thought that my soul – my wife's soul – our child's soul – all had been lost by my folly and sins of omission.... I might be unable to continue to work from feebleness ... and most painful of all that Polly might be left a widow with her little baby – unprotected by a father's care.

He is torn between the need for more money and the bad effect on him and his family of working such long hours and being away from home, particularly after the birth of his son.

I have taken stock and find that we have spent near £500 this past year. This will not do. We must retrench.... I have worked hard – travelled much – been little at home and lived a hurrying unsettled life, which has I fear had an evil influence both upon Polly and myself. With Polly it has led to dissatisfaction and occasional sourness of temper – to low points and ill health. With me it has brought about a degree of coarseness of manner and hastiness of temper, which I am ashamed of.... Wealth ... would be purchased at too costly a note if its acquisition led to a loss of the refinements of mind and gentleness of manner which I ought to strive to possess and exhibit especially at home.

The most anguished passages in the diaries describe the birth of his son. (Childbirth was dangerous for both mother and baby.) On the night of the birth his usual feelings of guilt mix with panic.

Tuesday 18 August 1846: 5 minutes to 10. My poor, dear little Polly is now in the midst of her trial. She bears it like a little heroine – nobly – as she does everything. She had a very bad night last night and tho' she 'sacked' her nurse, who came to see her this morning, she had to send for her this evening. I got home at 7 and found that there was no time to lose. I sent for Smith [that is the doctor] and as he did not come quickly I went down to Manchester and afterwards up to Milne Prestwich Wood [this was the local hospital] and fetched him from there.... Poor dear kind good little Polly. How I reproach myself for being the cause of this evil travail. Poor love – just in the middle of one of her pains – terrible agony – she told me to take care not to hurt myself by lifting the ottoman alone. Punish me, oh Lord.... 13 minutes past 11. Smith has just come downstairs. He says 'I may make myself quite easy' as there is no danger. Poor dear little Polly. I am the cause of thy distress – I – and yet I do not bear thy pains.... Smith says the child has a large head and there is not much room for it to come.... Smith at 12 came down and said things remained in status quo and he wished for help and instruments – I went off for Mr Heath and fetched him – after such anxiety and deliverature [sic] – nature did what was wanted and our son was born at half past 1 on Wednesday morning. When he came he was black in the face and insensible but he was brought round soon and to my great delight was crying lustily.

Edward had described his affection for Mary in several diary entries before their marriage: 'My beloved Polly has been here all week and therefore I have no misfortunes or unhappiness to record. She is an excellent little girl and I always feel happy when I am privileged with her presence.' After they are married he writes of: 'her kind courage and beautiful cheering expressions'. The passages where he now writes about his wife and his new son are tender and proud:

> Polly is lying asleep on the sofa and the baby is below – so I will take advantage of the stillness to think over the last year – and to record impressions which should have been put on paper as normal at the end of the year. Polly is much stronger and looks better and prettier decidedly than when she was married…. Our baby is very hearty and is now crowing and laughing on his mother's knee. She is playing with him…. Our baby is glorious and is really a noble little fellow. His mother says he shall be a clergyman…. Polly is good and kind, tho' she is naturally of quick feelings. I must confess myself to blame in most of our little family quarrels…. The baby was inoculated on March 17 and cut two teeth the same day, which are very sharp as my fingers can testify…. Alfred grows apace and is very sharp – talks like a little parrot and is beloved extremely of his grandsires and grandmamas…. I hope soon to be settled – to have a fixed home –and a fixed life and purpose and in quiet happiness and a steady performance of duty to lead at least a blameless life before God and man…. I feel we have more than our share of blessings – and this at a time when trade is depressed and the Irish starving and most people anxious and miserable.

The last diary entry that has survived was written on 28 January 1848. It is again full of self-criticism and good intentions: 'Morally and intellectually speaking I look back with shame at no improvements. The mind and heart become callous and hardened if not cultivated. I must set about this work – both on my own account and Polly and Alfred's – as without it all other works are vain.'

Edward's two 'lost' diaries provide an intimate insight into the feelings of someone who was going to become an apparently ruthless businessman.

Their tone is echoed by a later description which is graphic and – for the time – surprisingly frank.

Watkin had worked for the Trent Valley Railway for only six months when the company was swallowed up by the London and Birmingham Railway in April 1846. This resulted in a considerable profit for the shareholders, who were asked to come to his office to collect their cheques. At the last moment he discovered several errors in the accounts. In his book *A trip to the United States and Canada*, published in 1852, Watkin described what amounted to a nervous breakdown.

We set to work, and I was up the best part of one, and the whole of another, night. I was so anxious that I did not feel to want food. In the early morning of the day on which we were to begin paying off our shareholders, the books balanced. It was a clear, cold morning. I went out to a little barber's shop and got shaved. I did not feel in want of food – and took none. At ten o'clock shareholders began to arrive, got their cheques, and went away satisfied. About noon Mr. Henry Houldsworth, the father of the present member for Manchester, called for his cheque; and, chatting with him at the time, as I was making the upstroke of the letter H in 'Houldsworth', I felt as if my whole body was forced up into my head, and that was ready to burst. I raised my head, and this strange feeling went away. I thought, how strange! I tried again, the same feeling came again and again, till, with a face white as paper, that alarmed those about me, I fell forward on the desk. Water was given me; but I could not swallow it. I never lost entire consciousness; but I thought I was going to die. They put me into a carriage, and took me to the consulting room, in Mosley Street, of my old friend William Smith, the celebrated Manchester surgeon. He placed me on a sofa and asked me what it was. I whispered, 'Up all night – over-anxious – no food.' He gave me brandy and soda water, and a biscuit, and told me to lie still. I had never tasted this popular drink before. In about a quarter of an hour I felt better, got up, and said, 'Oh! I am all right now.' But Mr. Smith, nevertheless, ordered me to go home at once, go to bed, take a pill – I assume, a narcotic – which he gave me, and not to get up till he had seen me in the morning. I insisted on calling at the office. I felt able to go on with my work. But at the office, something in my looks induced them to send a faithful clerk with me in the cab to our house. I found afterwards that some of the clerks said, 'We shall never see him again.'

I was distressed at the thought of alarming my wife, who was not in a condition to be alarmed [She was expecting their first child]. So, with what little strength I had left, I rubbed my forehead, face, nose, lips, chin, with my clenched fist, to restore some slight colour. Entering our door, I said, 'I am rather worn out, and will go to bed. Up all night. Work done. Now, please, I will go to bed.'

So, after every affectionate care that a good wife could pay, I swallowed my narcotic pill – and slept, slept, slept – till, at eight in the morning, the sun was coming in, charmingly, through the windows. Nothing seemed to ail me. What weakness, what nonsense, said I. I felt as if I could trample weakness under foot. I like work, too. And I had a sort of shame of confessing myself incapable.

It is remarkable that Watkin wrote so honestly – and so publicly – about his inner demons. To brush off the whole incident, to feel ashamed and to carry on as before was typical of the time he lived in, when Englishmen were expected to hide their emotions, above all, feelings of weakness. In fact, he actually carried on suffering in private for a further five years, during which he continued to work excessive hours as he built up his career outside Manchester. By 1851, however, he could not continue any longer:

To be laid up in bed for a month with a violent disease is nothing. You are killed or cured; made better, and your illness forgotten even by yourself; or quietly laid under the dust of your mother earth. But to have, as it were, your whole 'mind, body, soul, and strength' turned, with a resistless fascination, into the frightened study of your own dreadful anatomy. To find your courage quail, not before real danger, but at phantoms and shadows – nay, actually at your own horrid self – to feel every act of life and every moment of business a task, an effort, a trial, and a pain. Sometimes to be unable to sleep for a week – sometimes to sleep, but, at the dead of night, to wake, your bed shaking under you from the violent palpitation of your heart, and your pillow drenched with cold sweat pouring from you in streams. But, worst of all, if you are of a stubborn, dogged, temper, and are blessed with a strong desire to 'get on' – to feel yourself unable to make some efforts at all, to find yourself breaking down before all the world in others, and to learn, at last, in consequence, almost to hate the half-dead and failing carcase tied to your still living will. This not for months only, but for YEARS. Years, too, in what ought to be your prime of manhood. I – a man, a matter-of-fact man, a plain, hard-headed, unimaginative man of business. In the last four years I have lived the life of a soul in purgatory or an inhabitant of the 'Inferno,' and though I have worked like a horse, determined, if possible, to rout out my evil genii – the wave of health has gradually receded, till, at last, an internal voice has seemed solemnly to say, 'Thus far shalt thou go and no farther.' The history of my derangements is told above in one word: that word is – OVERWORK.

That vivid description is the last we learn of the intimate feelings of the young, confident yet frightened and guilty Mr Edward Watkin. As all his other diaries were destroyed the private man vanishes from public view for almost forty years until he reappears as Sir Edward Watkin MP, the Railway King, when he publishes a tribute to his wife on her death in March 1888. We cannot know how much of the earlier sensitive man remained privately or whether years of successful business deals and the acquisition of great wealth had made him, as he often seemed to his enemies – and in that 1848 entry feared he might be becoming – 'callous and hardened'.

The break in 1845 with Absalom Watkin & Son and the dusty world of Manchester cotton in order to join the exciting new industry of the railways had been a turning point in Watkin's public life. Two years later, in 1847, he was fined 6s. and the current year's subscription for failing to attend meetings of the Manchester Literary Society. He resigned his membership. He had left the Manchester Years behind him. He was about to step onto a bigger and more exciting stage.

Chapter 4

Sniffing the Breeze

In 1846 the campaign by the Anti-Corn Law League, which had dominated Absalom's political work, brought him to the edge of national fame and introduced his son to what Cobden had called the vortex of political excitement, reached a triumphant conclusion. The Corn Laws were repealed. It was an astonishing victory, with repercussions that went far beyond the price of bread, vital though that was to the poorest of the poor. Prime Minister Robert Peel, who came from Bury, 8 miles to the north of Manchester, knew what life was like for the poor in the new industrial cities. Although he was a Tory he had come to accept the justice of the Anti-Corn Law League's case and in his speech moving the repeal he paid gracious tribute to Cobden in saying that it was his leadership and oratory that had led to victory for the reformers.

A month later Peel resigned. This split the Conservative Party and Peel and his followers formed a separate group in the Commons, called the 'Peelites'. (Peel's name was a fertile field for nicknames. In his earlier, anti-Catholic days he was known as 'Orange Peel'. When he was MP for Tamworth in the Midlands, his constituency included the railway where Edward Watkin first made his name, the Trent Valley, which was dubbed 'Peel's Railway'. He founded the first police force and the new policemen were dubbed the 'Peelers' or more commonly 'Bobbies' after his first name.) After Peel's death in 1850 in a riding accident the Peelites and the Whigs created the Liberal Party, which formed the main opposition to the Conservatives until it was replaced in the twentieth century by the Labour Party. One of the brightest of the Tory Peelite MPs who joined the new Liberal Party was William Ewart Gladstone, later to be four times prime minister of Great Britain and the greatest Liberal statesman of the Victorian age. He became a close friend of Edward Watkin and was a frequent guest at Rose Hill, though Sir Edward recalled in his later years that his own first major involvement in Manchester politics was at the age of 18, when he helped defeat Gladstone, who was the Tory candidate.

As soon as its victory had been achieved the League dissolved itself. It had existed nationally for only eight years, but it had achieved its single aim and brought down the government in the process. It was the most successful popular movement in British political history. Edward had played a significant part in the League's campaign through his organisation of the League's offshoot in the new factories and cotton mills and its stunning victory must have been heady for a young man flexing his muscles. He was present with his father at a celebration banquet in Manchester at midnight on 31 January in 1849, when repeal passed into law. A cheque for £18,000, a colossal amount for the time, was presented to Cobden but Edward reported that there was 'dissatisfaction' at what he described as its 'oneness'. Bright, Cobden's partner throughout the campaign, received nothing. Edward wrote: 'Bright naturally feels hurt at the almost utter forgetfulness of his name'. He notes in his diary that the previous September Cobden had been on the verge of giving up the Corn Laws fight because he had no money. Bright had raised £10,000, the equivalent of £1 million today, to give to him.

By the end of the Corn Laws campaign Edward's own career had moved on. Britain was in the middle of the frenzy called Railway Mania with companies being created then collapsing on a daily basis. (In 1845 over 600 bills to establish new railways were presented to Parliament in a single day.) He had quickly made his mark in his new post as secretary to the Trent Valley Railway (TVR). The TVR directors commented on their secretary's 'ability, integrity and industry' and referred to 'the mode in which the accounts had been kept', which had saved the company 'considerable expense'. Soon the TVR was absorbed into the London and Birmingham and after only three months that company in turn was taken over by the London and North Western Railway (LNWR), with Watkin appointed as one of its administrative secretaries. As that description of his breakdown shows, his hard work had been at the expense of his health. When his illness had become too severe for him to continue his juggling act, he was forced to take time off work. It is typical of his approach to life, however, that he spent the time visiting North America, studying the American political system and their railroads and writing a book. That was to sow the seeds of a new public life on the other side of the Atlantic.

The LNWR was the largest railway company in Britain and proud of its nickname 'The Premier Line'. (It took 25 per cent of all the railway receipts in Britain at the time.) Its main route from Scotland to London is today's West Coast main line but it included the original Liverpool and Manchester Railway, which Absalom Watkin had taken his family to see on that historic day in September 1830.

Watkin was now in the big league. He had even come to the notice of the prime minister, Lord Palmerston, who considered appointing him to sort out the administrative mess of the Crimean War after Robert Stephenson described him as 'one of the cleverest men going', but nothing came of this. By 1853 his reputation was so high that he was appointed to the major post of General Manager of another new railway, the Manchester, Sheffield and Lincolnshire (MSLR). He was to remain with that company until December 1900, three months before his death. The MSLR was a perfect match for Watkin. It too was young and ambitious, and the company gave him an incentive by tying his salary to the profits he could generate.

In a sign of Watkin's growing reputation, after only one year the MSLR was asked if it would release him to re-organise the largest railway in Canada, the Grand Trunk Railway. Not surprisingly the directors refused to release him. But it was a hint of what was to come seven years later, when he would again be headhunted to rescue the Grand Trunk.

Watkin's energy and appetite for success were so prodigious that at the same time as he was making a name in the railway industry, he was moving into two other fields. With John Bright and other reformers from the Corn Law campaign he founded and wrote for a new radical newspaper called the *Manchester Examiner*. Those same links almost led to his being selected in 1846 as a parliamentary candidate in a by-election in Stafford.

The sitting Conservative MP, Captain the Honourable S.T. Carnegie, had just been appointed as a government whip and under the parliamentary rules at the time was required to resign and stand for re-election. The Liberals had decided to put up a candidate in opposition to Carnegie and found one at short notice. What happened next was typical in what Charles Dickens called Eatanswill contests for parliamentary seats. It was only fourteen years since the great Reform Act and Stafford had a few years earlier come close to being disenfranchised because of corruption.

On hustings day all the candidates addressed not only the electors of Stafford but onlookers, by speaking from three wagons pushed together in the marketplace to form a platform. The proceedings were presided over by the Mayor of Stafford, who occupied the centre wagon with the Town Clerk. The report in *The Times* captures the flavour of the event:

> The sudden and unexpected retirement of Mr Lawrence Heyworth (the Liberal candidate) on Tuesday evening was the occasion of much disappointment, not only to his friends, but also to a large body of the poorer electors, who considered the present as a legitimate occasion for getting some drink at the expense of someone or other. It appears that Mr L. Hayworth is a teetotaller, and that he urged his objections to intoxicating drinks so strongly to his committee, that it was intimated to him an election could not be carried in Stafford without treating of some kind. Accordingly, Mr Heyworth left Stafford on Tuesday night, and this morning a letter was received by the committee, formally announcing that he could not contest the borough on such principles, and conveying his resignation. The market-place was filled with numbers of the lower class all the morning, who were eagerly awaiting the arrival of some new candidate. The appearance of a barrel of ale, which was distributed among the thirsty crowd, was hailed with much cheering, and satisfied the free and independent electors that 'something was up'.

In fact, two new Liberal candidates appeared, in addition to the retiring MP. One was Dr W.W. Sleigh. He was, however, a supporter of the Corn Laws and had form with Watkin. The two men had crossed swords at an unruly meeting in Manchester five years earlier, when Edward had been in the chair. (At the time Richard Cobden wrote Watkin a deliciously insulting letter about Dr Sleigh, in which he referred to a dinner that Sleigh had attended at Aylesbury, where the doctor 'was seized with a fit of uncontrollable acquisitiveness which led him to take the spoons and salt cellars'.) The other Liberal candidate was – according to *The Times* report – 'Mr Edmund Watkin, the son of Mr Absalom Watkin, a manufacturer of Manchester.' The report contains the full speeches of the three candidates. Watkin's was enthusiastically received and he was nominated and seconded with 'much cheering', in spite of the fact that he had just revealed that he was disqualified from standing for Parliament since he lacked the required minimum of £300 a year in landed property. (He said that the only property he owned was his hands and his head.) 'The Mayor then took the show of hands. The great majority of the meeting complied with the call in favour of Mr Watkins [*sic*], amid enthusiastic cheering and clapping of hands. The Mayor declared the show of hands to be in favour of Mr Watkin. (Cheers.)'

Captain Carnegie had revealed in his speech that he was now a supporter of the repeal of the Corn Laws. As a result, Watkin issued a statement urging his supporters to vote for the Captain. The election went ahead with only two candidates. Carnegie won by a landslide: 708 votes to Sleigh's 25.

The thrill of being immersed in party politics, of finding people wanted him to be an MP and the whiff of wheeler-dealing – something that always interested Watkin – must have been heady stuff for a 27-year-old, just becoming aware of the exciting powers that lay within him. It put down a marker for a parliamentary career which would eventually span almost half a century. But not yet.

For the next ten years Watkin's focus was on his career in the railways. After the birth of his daughter, Harriette, he was a family man with two young children. He needed a steady income, though there was no question of returning to his father's warehouse to sell calico. By 1857, though, Edward Watkin's parliamentary prospects could hardly have been more glittering. His CV included the prominent part he had played with his father in the Anti-Corn Law League, at first in Manchester, then more widely as national chairman of its off-shoot organisation for factory workers. He had shown himself to be a brilliant fundraiser by rescuing the Manchester Athenaeum from bankruptcy. He was making his name with the MSLR and the railways were by now the landmark industry of Victorian Britain. Even the prime minister had noticed him. He was a family man, young, energetic, a confident and skilled speaker and a published writer. And he had charisma. He also had the support of one of the most respected politicians in the country, Richard Cobden. The two men had become close. Cobden ended one letter to Watkin with: 'I shall be delighted to have a gossip with you. What say you to a cup of tea at 7 on Sunday?' (After Cobden's death Watkin published a reverential book called *Alderman Cobden of Manchester*.)

At the age of 38, he made his political move and was formally nominated as Liberal candidate for Yarmouth in a by-election. Cobden, who did not normally involve himself in elections, wrote him a warm personal letter of endorsement:

> Can I do anything to help you at Yarmouth? If so, I shall be glad to hear from you. Having had you for a colleague when you were in your teens and watched you ever since I take great interest in your present undertaking. We want some men of your age and active energies in the House, and without flattery I predict for you both in debate and committees a useful career. The misfortune is generally that men of business come into Parliament too late in life, after their powers are exhausted; but you having secured an honourable independence early in life and having wisely resolved to apply your talents to the public service will I feel convinced have a successful career.

High praise from a great man. Sadly, Watkin failed to live up to it.

The campaign went well. Watkin won the election and became an MP in March 1857. But his first parliamentary term had lasted only four months when his opponents petitioned against the result, alleging corruption. In August a parliamentary committee found that some of Watkin's supporters had indeed bribed electors. Although the committee cleared Watkin himself of corruption, the election was declared invalid and he was unseated. In the general election of 1859 he fought the seat again but the whiff of corruption had tarnished him and he lost heavily.

It was a serious setback for such an ambitious man, and it was a further five years before he stood for Parliament again, though he did serve one term of three years as a Manchester councillor. (The possibility of standing locally for election had been mentioned sixteen years earlier, in 1846, when the *Manchester Guardian* reported that 'Mr Edward Watkin, who was so well and favourably known to the public, also would not object to being a councillor.') Becoming a councillor was probably a way of keeping his political hand in while he was looking round for another constituency and in 1864 he stood for Stockport (Cobden's first seat) at a by-election on the death of the previous MP, who had succeeded Cobden in 1847. As was allowed in those days, Cobden had stood in the general election that year in the West Riding of Yorkshire as well as in Stockport. He won in both but must have thought the Yorkshire seat a better bet since he chose it rather than Stockport. In the 1864 by-election Watkin was returned unopposed but in the general election the following year he came top of the poll of three candidates.

Shortly before the 1868 general election, he was so confident of being returned that he offered 'his' seat to Gladstone in gratitude for the way the party leader had supported him the previous year when Watkin had faced a rumour of having accepted bribes. In 1868 Gladstone was the member for the marginal seat of South Lancashire and was defeated there by 300 votes. Fortunately – as in Cobden's case – he had also stood for Greenwich and been returned with a large majority there. Ironically, Watkin was defeated in Stockport by 60 votes.

During his time as the MP for Stockport a bill came before the Commons to give the vote to working-class men. Watkin was one of only seventy-eight MPs who tried to substitute the word 'persons' for the word 'men'. In other words, to give women the vote. He was sixty-one years ahead of his time. Six years after his defeat in Stockport he was elected as MP for Hythe, a constituency he represented for twenty-one years. He was an MP – with interruptions – from 1857 to 1895.

Notably early in his parliamentary career his potential was recognised when he was appointed chairman of two financial sub-committees. But that was the limit of his achievements in the House of Commons. Chasing success in other fields, above all in the railways, meant that he never lived up to Cobden's high hopes for him as a parliamentarian.

Watkin's achievements in the 1840s, 50s and 60s would have been enough even for an unusually ambitious man in Victorian Britain. But his desire for success and the fame that goes with it was not sated. Two years after taking over as chairman of the MSLR in 1864 he was appointed chairman of the South Eastern Railway (SER). The energy and business acumen needed to develop both of these companies were enormous, particularly since – as we shall see in a later chapter – he had plans to expand them as part of a scheme to create a railway to Paris and eventually India.

But all Watkin's grand schemes in Britain pale in comparison with what would be his most impressive triumph, his role in the creation of the Dominion of Canada, which began when he was 'headhunted' for the second time to rescue a bankrupt railway in what was called at the time British North America.

Chapter 5

Canada – Birth of a Nation

A public life that had started during the Manchester Years was to lead to Edward Watkin's name being recognised throughout the world. Arguably the most significant stage in that journey began in 1861, when he rescued the Grand Trunk Railway of Canada from disaster. His activities in British North America – the province of Canada was only one part – lasted eight years since they concerned something far greater than sorting out a railway. He was asked by the British Cabinet to take part in the negotiations to create a new country. What makes this turning point in his career extraordinary for someone who loved the limelight – self-publicity had always been a feature of his portfolio – was that because of the need for confidentiality much of the work had to be carried out in secret. One writer has called it 'one of the most puzzling episodes in his career'. As a result, and in spite of the knighthood given to him by a grateful government when he finally returned to the UK, his work in Canada has never received the recognition it deserves.

When Watkin became involved in its affairs the Grand Trunk, the biggest railway in British North America, had just revealed debts of $72 million and was about to collapse. *The Times* of London thundered: 'No single event in the history of finance has ever caused such wide-spread anxiety as now prevails regarding this undertaking.' The company was virtually bankrupt, its profits drained by inefficiency and years of lining the pockets of local and national politicians. In July 1861 the Grand Trunk shareholders published a stark report. It described the state of the railway as so disastrous as to 'render hope and confidence impossible' and continued: 'This great property has come to be regarded almost as a hopeless wreck, driven to and fro by every evil influence.' What was needed was that 'in order to straighten out the Company's affairs … a man of great skill, experience and energy should proceed at once to Canada. This man would take over the entire supervision of the Company and negotiate with the Government.' The directors of the Grand Trunk acted immediately by announcing the appointment of 'Mr Watkin, the general manager of the Manchester, Sheffield and Lincolnshire Railway, as a proper person to be entrusted with the entire supervision of the affairs of the company in Canada, and especially to conduct the negotiations with the Government (there).' If what had gone before had not made clear how desperate the situation was, the next sentence did: 'Arrangements have been made for Mr Watkin to proceed to Canada in the course of a week or two.'

The timing of Watkin's appointment was curious. Because of his heavy workload at the MSLR his health had been suffering. The directors had just granted him three months' leave of absence to recover and a gift equivalent to £40,000. He actually took the job in Canada while he was on sick leave.

The prospect before him would have been daunting for most people but for someone with Watkin's temperament it was an exhilarating challenge. The company's name had become a byword for corruption. Thousands of dollars' worth of equipment was lying unused at depots. Jobs were ill-defined and duplicated. The Freight Traffic Manager was an 'unmitigated scoundrel', who had been fixing the train fares to encourage passengers to use his own steamboats instead of the railway. An anonymous letter sent to the directors pulled no punches and named names:

> Yates is said to have withdrawn £70000 from company accounts. Waddell resides in the same house as Mr Hickson. Ask if Mr Hickson is not the owner of a racehorse known by the name of Bella. Directors cannot be aware of the enormous losses sustained by the company by the destruction of engines and cars by collisions, running off lines, by Robbery, Defalcation [i.e. misappropriation of funds], destruction of firewood stacked on the line by Fire, etc, etc.

Watkin was sometimes accused of failing to follow up details and it is true that his love of thinking big and what we would call 'outside the box' could be a weakness as well as a strength. Magdalen Goffin wrote that he thought 'in large intuitive sweeps' and one of the more elegant obituaries written about him said that he had a genius for innovation, a gentle way of saying that he did not always complete what he started. With the Grand Trunk, however, he probed forensically into the dark corners and swept away the cobwebs with his new broom. He found the company 'an organised mess, led by a rascally element'. He cut the workforce drastically, including sacking half the engineers, who he said spent most of their time on experiments instead of dealing with urgent day-to-day problems. One experimenter during company time was a young telegraph operator. He had asked to work the night shift just so that he would have plenty of time to carry out his own experiments during the quiet hours. One night he was working with a battery that spilled sulphuric acid onto the floorboards, ate its way through the ceiling onto his boss's desk below and destroyed some important papers on it. He was fired the next morning. By the time of his death in 1931, however, he had taken out over 2,000 patents, including the world's first phonograph, light bulb and motion picture projector. His name was Thomas Eddison.

Watkin's efforts were dramatically successful. Within a year the Grand Trunk's profits had increased by 60 per cent and by October 1862 the board was so pleased with his work that they made him president of the company. By 1869 he had not only rescued the Grand Trunk's fortunes, he had developed it into the longest railway in the world.

But that task, mammoth though it was, proved in the end to be a side issue to his political work in Canada.

In 1862 what we now call Canada was formed of six British colonies, officially united under the Crown as British North America, but in practice independent of each other. To the south it shared a border with the United States of America, which had been an independent country for less than a century and was fighting a civil war. But once that war was over, the USA was hungry to take territory from its neighbour, which was too fragmented politically to defend itself. British North America was in reality only a geographical entity, though its statistics were remarkable. It contained 7 per cent of the earth's total land mass, second only in size to Russia and stretching from the Arctic in the north to the United States in the south, from the Pacific Ocean in the west to the Atlantic in the east. Snow lay for six to nine months a year over much of the territory and its far north was covered in permafrost. In the second half of the nineteenth century its roads and canals were unusable in the winter and it lacked the mark of every developing country at the time: a railway network. In 1850 Britain had 6,000 miles of track. The United States had 9,000 miles. British North America had 68 miles. Large tracts were wilderness, with only a few centres of population. Winnipeg and Vancouver did not even exist.

At many points in his career Watkin showed a genius for recognising potential. This was one. He saw the tremendous commercial possibilities of the railways in Canada and after his re-organisation of the existing Grand Trunk network he set about expanding it. Trains, able to travel enormous distances in all seasons, could break the stranglehold that extreme weather and geography had always held on Canada. Even before he arrived in Canada he had had a vision of the importance of trains to the territory but not just as a means of transport. He saw them as the key to Canada's political development. The vision of a railway joining the west and east coasts of the continent of America had gripped him and he had written an article in 1861 for the *Illustrated London News* with the title: 'A British Railway from the Atlantic to the Pacific'. He was right in his vision. One historian wrote: 'Without railways there would be and could be no Canada.'

Watkin was lucky in his timing. It chimed with the concerns of a powerful politician 4,000 miles away in the Mother Country, the British Colonial Secretary, the splendidly named Henry Pelham Fiennes Pelham-Clinton, 5th Duke of Newcastle-under-Lyme.

When Richard Cobden and the Anti-Corn Law League brought down the government of Sir Robert Peel in 1846, one of the Tories who became a Peelite and later transferred his allegiance to the new Liberal Party was Henry Pelham-Clinton. From 1859 to 1864 he served in Lord Palmerston's Liberal administration as Colonial Secretary and was a member of the Cabinet. In 1860 he went with the Prince of Wales to British North America and the United States and discovered at first-hand how vulnerable to invasion the British provinces were.

The Duke and the Prince were not alone in their fears. John McDonald, who was to become the first prime minister of a united Canada in 1867, wrote earlier: 'I would be quite willing, personally, to leave that whole country a wilderness for the next half century but I fear that if Englishmen do not go there, Yankees will.' Back in 1812 America had invaded part of British North America in a war that lasted three years but settled no territorial disputes. A bill was introduced in the American House of Representatives at the time, calling for the annexation of British North America and the admission of its provinces as states and territories of the United States. A report to the Revenue Commissioners of the United States in 1866 said: 'If the Maritime Provinces [of Britain] would join us spontaneously today … they would greatly strengthen and improve our position, and aid us in our struggle for equality upon the ocean. If we would succeed upon the deep we must either maintain our fisheries or ABSORB THE PROVINCES.'

Watkin's involvement with the Grand Trunk Railway coincided with a point in the history of North America that spelt particular danger to the British provinces. His outstanding work in building up the Grand Trunk fitted perfectly into the Duke's own aim to develop a railway built exclusively on British territory. (Many of the railways at the time crossed the border into the United States.) This would not only improve trade within British North America. It would enable the rapid transport of soldiers and military equipment in the event of war. Crucially, it would also focus the minds of the independent provinces on the need for unity.

The paths of the Duke and Edward Watkin had first crossed in 1845 when Watkin and the Mayor of Manchester had gone to Downing Street to ask the prime minister, Sir Robert Peel, for money to finance the first public parks in the town. The Duke was at the time the First Commissioner of Woods and Forests. He had urged Peel to refuse a grant, saying that if money was given to Manchester for parks every town would want a slice of the cake. In 1847 Watkin met the Duke again, who although the son of a peer was entitled to stand as an MP. Watkin was part of a deputation that persuaded him to stand down in favour of John Bright as candidate for the new borough of Manchester. In 1852 Watkin was on the train to Derby when he noticed a man reading his new book, *A trip to the United States and Canada*. It was the Duke. They talked about American politics. Two years later it was the Duke who turned down Lord Palmerston's suggestion that Watkin should be asked to sort out the mess in the Crimea, but the two men met again in 1857. A MSLR locomotive had set fire to one of the Duke's plantations. Watkin, who was by now the Manager of the MSLR, went to see the Duke, who had written to the company in what Watkin described as 'a very haughty manner'. Watkin wrote about their meeting:

I waited some time; but at last in stalked the Duke, looking very awful indeed – so stern and severe – that I could not help smiling and saying, 'The burnt coppice, your Grace.' Upon this he laughed, held out his hand, placed me beside him, and we had a very long discussion, not about the fire … but about Canada, the United States, and the Colonies generally.

Not many people in that deferential age would have dared react to a stern duke by smiling but Watkin was not easily abashed.

The Duke and Watkin realised that they shared the concept of a great new railway in British North America. The Duke later read Watkin's article in the *Illustrated London News*. In his book *Canada and the States*, published in 1887, Watkin looked back to a key meeting he had with the Duke:

> Prior to my sailing to New York, en route for Canada, to fulfil my mission for the Grand Trunk, I had a long interview with the Duke of Newcastle, as Colonial Minister. He had seen, and we had often previously discussed, the questions raised in my article. Every point connected with the British Provinces in America, as affected by the then declared warlike separation of the northern and southern portions of the United States, was carefully discussed. The Duke had the case at his fingers' ends. The Intercolonial Railway, to connect Halifax on the Atlantic with the Grand Trunk Railway at Riviere du Loup, 106 miles below Quebec, he described as 'the preliminary necessity.' He authorized me to say, in Canada, that the Colonial Office would pay part of the cost of surveys; that these works must be carried out in the greatest interests of the nation, and that he would give his cordial help. From that day in July, 1861, I regarded myself as the Duke's unofficial, unpaid, never-tiring agent in these great enterprises.

The knighthood Watkin was offered by the British government at the end of the negotiations in 1868 is proof of the importance of his role in the creation of the Dominion. That role is evidenced further in the extensive correspondence between him and the Duke which is available in the archives of Nottingham University. In a letter to the Duke sent in September 1861 from Quebec, Watkin reports on his negotiations with 'leading members of the Governments of Canada' (i.e. the separate provinces). He has arranged 'to send a delegation from each Province to England, without delay, to negotiate with your Grace and the [British] Government'. In February 1862 he writes during one of his boat journeys round Canada to say that what he has negotiated will 'get rid of one of Mr Gladstone's "practical objections"'. (Gladstone was Chancellor of the Exchequer at the time.) Another letter shows Watkin's confidence in his role: 'I have made another representation to Gladstone to urge the US Government to modify their restrictions. What I want is for him to address an earnest remonstrance to Washington <u>and do it now</u>.' The curt underlining is Watkin's.

There is a further reference to Gladstone in a letter written the same year from the Euston Hotel in London. Watkin has just had a meeting in Liverpool with Joseph Howe, the premier of Nova Scotia, one of the Canadian provinces, and Samuel Tilley, the premier of another, New Brunswick. Watkin writes: 'The Honourable Mr Howe will stay a day or two with Mrs Watkin and myself. He is anxious to have an unofficial conversation with Mr Gladstone at once. I have promised to go with him, and we will take the Hon Mr Tilley, who is also here, with us.'

That letter is an example of one of Watkin's special skills. One commentator said of his work in Canada: 'None knew better the art of getting men together.' A journalist once called Watkin 'the master of the judicious lunch'. It was in a string of informal social meetings as well as in formal negotiations that Watkin made his impact in Canada. One month after he took up his post with the Grand Trunk Railway he organised a dinner party in Montreal for representatives of five of the British North American provinces to discuss a railway to link them. During the evening the prime minister of Nova Scotia said: 'There are men in this room who hold the destinies of half of the Continent in their hands and yet we never meet. We have done more good by a free talk over the table tonight than all the governors, general and local, could do in a year.' When a dinner was held in 1867 for the delegates to a conference set up to examine the bill establishing the new Canada, Watkin was its chairman. In his book *Colony to Nation*, Arthur Lower reviews the personalities involved in establishing the Dominion of Canada and writes: 'A few dwarf all others.' He selects five Canadians and three Englishmen as the stars. The English are Sir Edmund Walter Head, the Governor-General of the original Canada from 1854 to 1861, the Duke of Newcastle and Edward Watkin. The Canadian writer, Professor Andy den Otter, names Watkin as one of three 'Philosophers' who guided the Canadian railway system. (He also quotes approvingly the *Railway Times* magazine calling Watkin 'romantic and adventurous' – a good description of the attractive side of Watkin's character.) Another Canadian writer says of Watkin: 'He had an appreciation of colonial issues not general in England.' He made frequent speeches in the House of Commons in support of Canadian Federation. During the three years in which he was a Manchester councillor (before he moved back to Parliament) he spoke at four public meetings in Liverpool and the Manchester area about the need for a railway between two of the Canadian provinces. He even persuaded Manchester Council to pass a formal resolution that must have been unusual for the city: 'That a memorial be presented by this Council to her Majesty's Government to co-operate with the governments of Canada, New Brunswick and Nova Scotia ... to secure the construction of a railway communication between Quebec and Halifax'.

One other story shows how close a relationship Watkin developed with the leading politicians of Canada. When honours were being distributed at the end of the successful negotiations for a unified Canada, George Etienne Cartier, the leader of Quebec Province, was offered only a Companionship of the Order of the Bath. Watkin had been offered a knighthood but declined because of what he saw as an injustice to Cartier, who had worked hard with him to overcome the suspicions that the French-speaking province of Quebec had about the British. He only accepted his own knighthood the following year, when Cartier was also receiving a knighthood. Cartier wrote to a friend that Watkin was defeated in Protestant Stockport because he had laid the cornerstone of a Roman Catholic school and drunk the health of the Pope.

All this evidence shows how important a player Watkin was in the formation of the Dominion of Canada. However, one further and dramatic initiative by him stands out in the history of that country: his negotiations to purchase the vast territory owned by the Hudson's Bay Company in the centre and the north of Canada. Without that sale the massive expansion of the railway west on its way to the Pacific would never have happened.

After one of his earlier meetings with the Duke of Newcastle, Watkin wrote: 'I called the Duke's special attention to the position and attitude of the Hudson's Bay authorities. How they were always crying down their territory as unfit for settlement; repelling all attempts from the other side to open up the land by roads, and to use steamers on such grand rivers as, for instance, the Assinboine and the Saskatchewan.'

Since 1670 the Hudson's Bay Company (originally established under Royal Charter as 'The Governor and Company of Adventurers of England trading into Hudson's Bay') had had the monopoly of all trade in Rupert's

Land, which stretched north to the Arctic Circle from the more populated areas bordering the Atlantic Ocean. The territory was named after Prince Rupert of the Rhine, a nephew of Charles I, and the first Governor of the Hudson's Bay Company. In December 1821 the Company's monopoly was extended west to the Pacific coast and it became the biggest landowner in the world. The area was larger than European Russia, but much of it was snowbound. Its sole produce was furs, which the Company bought from native Indian trappers and sold at great profit. Its 286 shareholders, all living in England, received a lucrative annual dividend, usually 10 to 15 per cent.

For many years – as Watkin wrote in his letter to the Colonial Secretary – the Company had portrayed their territory as an icy desert, suitable only for native fur trappers and incapable of sustaining a road network, travel by steamers or settlement. But Watkin did not accept this. In his *Illustrated London News* article he had written that the British territory from the Atlantic to the Pacific, including some of the land owned by the Hudson's Bay Company, was 'within the wheat-growing line'. Its potential was vast and could only be tapped by the building of a railway through it. The Hudson's Bay Company was in the way. Watkin asked the British and Canadian governments to buy the company out. The Duke took his proposal to the British Cabinet but failed to convince them that there would be sufficient return for their money. The government of the original province of Canada followed the lead of the Mother Country and also refused.

The decisions of the two governments would have daunted an ordinary man. But they came up against Watkin's refusal to be beaten, what you might call – after the donations for the restoration of St Wilfrid's Church in Northenden – Watkin's ninepence. The details of what he achieved can be found in a minute book in the archives of Hull University. It describes in dry terms a dramatic financial negotiation with Watkin at its centre.

The Duke had started the process off when he told the Governor of the Hudson's Bay Company that their attitude must change, specifically that 'communication across the territory of the Company must be improved'. That was Watkin's way in, a nod in his direction, what men in Victorian times used to call 'a glimpse of a well-turned ankle'. On one of his Atlantic crossings a few months later he had told his friend Thomas Baring, the banker: 'We must make the matter go, now.' (Always a man of action, in his original magazine article proposing a railway across Canada, he had asked: 'How is this hope to be realised, not a century hence, but in our time?')

Andrew Smith (*British Businessmen and Canadian Confederation* (McGill-Queen's University Press, 2008)) describes the process by which Canada became united as having been shaped by 'gentlemanly capitalists' such as Watkin, whom he identifies as 'a powerful new force'. Professor Ian Wray (*Great British Plans – Who Made Them and How They Worked* (Routledge, 2016)) sees Watkin as one of a breed of dynamic 'civic entrepreneurs' who are the essential key to turning great plans into reality. Smith goes on to say that, 'Watkin was consistently modest in talking about his role in bringing about Canadian Confederation' and emphasises the major part he played in facilitating dealings between the Colonial Secretary and the colonists.

In February 1862 Watkin formed, together with Baring, a pressure group in London called the British North American Association. Its stated aim was to create an umbrella large enough for anyone to shelter under: 'to enable the imperial and colonial interests on both sides of the Atlantic to confer on all topics of mutual interest'. The BNAA's membership included many of the key figures in the City and seventeen MPs. Watkin and Baring were members of its Governing Council. A month later the directors of the Hudson's Bay Company were invited to join the association, a move that had Watkin's fingerprints all over it. Doubtless, many judicious lunches followed.

The next significant step involved the newly formed International Finance Society. The purpose of the Society was what it said on the tin, to provide funds for large international deals. It was established on 11 May 1863 and at its first meeting eleven days later the sole item on the agenda (and the main item at all its meetings over the next five weeks, according to its minute book at Hull University) was 'A proposal from Mr Edward Watkin and friends to purchase the Hudson's Bay Company'. Shortly after that inaugural meeting Watkin met the Duke in private for 2 hours.

Incredibly, just over three weeks later the sale had been completed and on 26 June Thomas Baring wrote to the Duke to say that terms had been agreed. The price was £1.5 million, twice the value of the company at the time. Someone, surely Watkin, had done an amazing selling job on a group of hard-headed financiers. A prospectus was issued almost immediately with a deadline for applications just over a week later, at noon on 8 July. The timings make it obvious that the whole process had been co-ordinated in the background well before the prospectus had been issued. The speed and the scale of a speculative operation that had been rejected by the British and the Province of Canada's governments were breathtaking. The £1.5 million price in 1863 is the equivalent of £120 million today.

The closing words of Baring's letter to the Duke echo the wording of the agenda item at the International Finance Society's first meeting and show what had been happening behind the scenes: 'The whole of the interests of the Hudson's Bay Company are to be transferred to parties represented by Edward Watkin.' All the references to the deal in the Finance Society's minutes are to 'Mr Edward Watkin and friends'. He was at the centre of what was by any standards an astonishing deal.

It is striking proof of Watkin's skill as a negotiator and the confidence in him at the highest level that he carried out such a pivotal role. But his part did not end with the signing of the deal. The share prospectus concludes: 'For this, as well as for other proposed objects, Mr Edward Watkin, who is now in Canada, will be commissioned … to visit the Red River and southern districts, to consult the officers of the Company there, and to report as to the best and safest means of giving effect to the contemplated operations.' After the drama of perhaps the greatest financial deal of the age the directors of the new company needed someone to get down to the nitty-gritty of the practical details. Watkin the visionary became Watkin the man with the rolled-up sleeves.

But visionary he was. The prospectus paints a glowing picture of the future now that the plan for a cross-Canada railway had become a reality: European colonisation, mining, telegraphic links with the Pacific Coast, with Japan and Asia waiting just beyond. One newspaper, writing nearly a quarter of a century later, on the opening of the Canadian Pacific Railway in 1887, reminded its readers that Watkin was one of the first advocates of a British railway from the Atlantic to the Pacific. The article concludes: 'According to the view taken by Sir Edward, Canada must become the great highway to the rest of the Empire and its East. The mails to Australia at present go by way of New York and San Francisco. Sir Edward contends that at some near date they should be sent by way of Halifax and Vancouver.'

Back in 1863 the Canadian newspapers had no doubt who had taken the leading role in the Hudson's Bay negotiations. The *Toronto Globe* called Watkin 'a plenipotentiary to the Canadian Government' and the *Ontario London Free Press* reported a rumour that Watkin was going to set up a new country based on the Hudson's Bay territory and make himself king. A grateful International Finance Company rewarded him with £70,000 in shares (the equivalent of over £500,000 today).

The sale of the Hudson's Bay Company – the missing link between British Columbia, bordering the Pacific Ocean, and the provinces on the Atlantic seaboard – was a turning point in the establishment of the new Dominion of Canada. Douglas McKay, the official historian of the Hudson's Bay Company, has described it as: 'the greatest transfer of a territory ever accomplished unheralded by war'. Watkin's key role in the sale was a testament to his grasp of both the big and the small pictures, his inter-personal skills and his refusal to be beaten.

On 1 July 1867 the separate provinces became the united Dominion of Canada. Clause 145 of its first constitution must be unique for a constitution setting up a new country. It states that the construction of a railway system was 'essential to the Consolidation of the Union of British North America'. The building blocks of what eventually became the national Canadian railway network were the Grand Trunk, the Intercolonial Railway and finally the greatest engineering feat in a century of great engineering: the Canadian Pacific Railway, 3,400 miles long, crossing the Rockies at Kicking Horse Pass, 5,339ft (1,617m) above sea level and realising the dream of joining the Atlantic and the Pacific Oceans. But it was Watkin's expanded Grand Trunk Railway that led the way. As one writer said, the development of the Grand Trunk Railway by Watkin, which transformed it into the longest railway in the world, was one of the main factors that pushed British North America towards Confederation. It showed what was possible. One Canadian academic has written that he presents his students with an image of Edward Watkin and reclaims him as one of Canada's founders.

Watkin's achievements in Canada, both in rescuing the Grand Trunk Railway and in his top-level political work, show him at his most effective, pursuing a grand vision, wheeler-dealing on the details and massaging (sometimes bullying) key people. In order to achieve what he did, however, including his rescue and expansion of what *The Times* had only a few years before called the 'hopeless wreck' of the Grand Trunk Railway, Watkin spent an incredible amount of time and energy in British North America. The convenience of 7-hour flights by jet plane was a century away in the future. Each journey across the Atlantic took ten days. By October 1869 he was exhausted. He declined to stand again as President of the Grand Trunk and returned to Britain. What he left behind, however, was literally and metaphorically an iron thread that eventually linked two oceans and united a new country.

When Disraeli, Watkin's political opponent, gave him a knighthood in 1868, the *Guardian* published an editorial about his work in creating the new Canada: 'In the carrying out of the plan of confederation of the British North American provinces no man rendered greater service to the Colonial Ministers and leading members of the present and former Governments than Sir Edward', and added: 'He won in a very remarkable manner the confidence and esteem of the local Governments.'

Watkin always found the North American continent exciting. He wrote in 1887, long after his work for the Dominion was over, that he had the previous year completed his thirtieth crossing of the Atlantic Ocean as he had begun, as a tourist.

His work for Canada remains his greatest international legacy and perhaps what made him most proud. In 1887 his portrait was hung in the Royal Academy. It shows him holding a piece of paper in his hand. On it is written the single word 'Canada'.

Chapter 6

Edward and Absalom – Their Last Years Together

Watkin's appointment as Superintending Commissioner of the Grand Trunk Railway in July 1861 marked the start of the period of his greatest achievements. Sadly, his father, who died in the December, lived only just long enough to see Edward begin to prove the truth of what he had written about his 8-year-old son in 1827: 'He will assuredly prove superior to the herd of mankind.'

Happily though, Absalom's last years had seen a change in his spiky relationship with his son. We can see from several brief entries in Absalom's diaries how Edward had begun to assume the senior decision-making role within the family – August 1846: 'Consulted Mr Smith, the surgeon, at the desire of Edward.' May 1849: 'Sat for my portrait, by Edward's desire.' In September 1849 Absalom became a director of a new railway company, 'on Edward's proposal'. In January 1850 Absalom asked Edward's advice on what to do about the relationship between his daughter, Elizabeth, and W.H. Mellor, a dallying suitor, and again in April 1851: 'I wrote at Edward's suggestion a soothing letter to Elizabeth.' In March 1853 Edward arranged for Absalom to have a railway pass so that he could visit friends in Dover. December 1855: 'Mr Smith, the surgeon, was brought here by Edward at noon.'

After a consultation arranged 'at the desire of Edward', the doctor advised Absalom that he needed 'rest, relaxation and sea air'. Edward acted fast and the next day he and his father set off for Fleetwood by train. The visit was a great success. 'A pleasant journey of three hours and a half. Edward had engaged a very pleasant sitting room and bedroom for me at the North Euston Hotel.' (The hotel still bears the same name, recalling the days when the west coast railway line ended at Fleetwood, with passengers who had got on the train at Euston Station in London having to finish the journey to Glasgow by boat.) In the 1850s the hotel was only for the wealthy. A sitting room cost 3s. 4d. (16.5p) a day, and a bedroom was 2s. 3d. or 4s. 0d. (11p or 20p). Absalom continues:

> Fleetwood exceeded my expectation. It is well situated, and has the air of a thriving, well-built and well-planned seaport. It is not large but lively, and yet not disagreeably noisy. The walk along the shore is pleasant, and the sea breeze dry and agreeable. We walked a good deal, read Boswell's Johnson and were in bed by 11. I slept well and did not awaken till between 7 and 8, nor did I rise till after 8.

In September 1848 the two men set off for a week's tour together down south. They went first to London then to Ashbrittle, the Somerset village where Absalom's mother was born, and back to London. The trip with Edward was such a success that a year later they went back to Ashbrittle and had a tea 'with clouted [sic] cream'.

Those trips with Edward were among the furthest Absalom ever took. He was not a Victorian. He lived under George III, George IV and William IV and was 50 years old when Victoria became queen in 1837. He was nearly 60 before train travel became the norm and the railway must have seemed a marvel to him. At the end of the first trip with Edward he records that the journey home from London to Stockport took 5 hours. When he visited London with two friends in 1818 the same journey had taken 28½ hours. He never travelled outside Britain.

On 12 January 1855 Absalom's diary showed for the first time that his health was deteriorating:

> All day chilled, having a heavy pain at the top and on the left side of my face. I do not seem able to move readily or to turn my attention easily from one subject to another. At night I perceived that my fingers had not, on the left side, the power of contracting readily or forcibly. I could not grasp anything with the fingers of the hand, so as to hold it firmly.

It was the first of the strokes that seven years later would lead to his death.

On 28 June in the same year he writes: 'I could not arrange the cards in my hand and play with precision.' A further stroke in 1859 left him paralysed. Edward and his wife sold their house in nearby Timperley and came to live at Rose Hill, where they could better care for his father. The close relationship between Mary and Absalom (she got on well with

Edward's mother too) must have been a great relief to Watkin, who had grown up with such strains in his family. In a description of his wife's last hours (the third-person style is typical of the time) Edward wrote:

> During the afternoon she said: 'I am sure Grandpa is waiting to meet me.' She referred to Mr Absalom Watkin, her husband's father, between whom and herself there had existed, since the time of her marriage, a strong mutual affection; and whom she had tended during the last years of his life, when he was helpless and paralyzed; and when, often, she alone, guided by the fine instinct of loving sympathy, could interpret the feeble signs which served him for speech.

Edward's distress at his father's death and the stained glass window in St Wilfrid's Church have already been referred to. He commissioned another window in memory of his father in the parish church at Ashbrittle in Somerset, the village where his grandmother was born. It is next to one commissioned by him in memory of his grandmother.

Edward loved his grandmother, Betty. 'I knew my grandmother well; we learned as children order and neatness from her. She had a strong love of truth, hated a sham, and detested a lie.' Betty died in July 1830 and Magdalen Goffin writes of her funeral:

> Absalom wished his mother to be buried at Prestwich, by the church whose bells rang out over the brook to Broughton. He walked there with Edward but was refused permission; only those who lived in that parish could lie in that churchyard. She would have to be buried a little farther to the east, at Cheetham Hill, a village two miles from Manchester, a pleasant place of green fields and lanes, half-timbered farmsteads and a handful of comfortable houses built by rich merchants.

St Mark's Church had been open only thirty-six years when Betty Watkin was buried there but time has moved on in Cheetham Hill, which is now a built-up and run-down part of Manchester. The church was declared redundant and demolished in 1998. Its churchyard is fenced off and its entrance gates are padlocked. All the graves are overgrown with moss and weeds but Betty's – she is alone in the grave – has been found and cleaned.

Thirteen years after Absalom's death Edward wrote two appreciations of his father's character. They were printed privately and only a few copies have survived. What they contain shows the affection and respect that Edward developed as he and his father grew older. He wrote sensitively and with great insight about his father's depression. He described Absalom in Manchester as a 'a lone, bashful and melancholy boy' and wrote: 'How far his own father's long, slow illness and death; the break-up of his home, his mother's loneliness and struggle, affected the bias of his mind I can only conjecture.' One particularly vivid phrase captures this side of his father, when he refers to a 'streak of sadness' in Absalom.

In the first of his appreciations Edward describes his anger at a speech Lord Derby had made which contained a number of derogatory remarks about black men. He uses it as a basis for drawing a contrast between the aristocrat and Absalom:

> Yesterday I read Lord Derby's speech at Liverpool in which he declaimed against 'coating with moral whitewash' the race of 'black men'. Hence I feel stirred afresh to give to a circle of relatives and friends an insight into the life of a man who was neither a lord nor a philosopher, but simply a Christian, who believed in Christianizing all men, whether black or white; a man, who as a scholar was erudite; as a speaker, always able, and at times eloquent; as a politician, enlightened; but still a man who only now and again emerged into the sight and hearing of the great world.

The paragraph avoids the floweriness of many Victorian eulogies and is a fine example of Edward's ability with words. It contains a shrewd assessment of Absalom. In calling his father 'enlightened' and a 'politician' Edward uses two words that he would have been proud to see applied to himself. His reference to Absalom as a public speaker being 'always able and at times eloquent' is spot on in its carefully balanced qualifications. The striking description of his father as 'a man who only now and again emerged into the sight and hearing of the great world' captures one of the most distinctive features of Absalom's elusive, will-o'-the-wisp character. It is Edward's final judgement on a man who had exerted such a strong influence on him, for good and bad.

One year after Absalom died Edward erected a memorial to him on the terrace of Rose Hill. It is a simple stone block, inscribed with the important dates of Absalom's life and death and scriptural quotations, and would have been seen by all those important visitors to the house in Edward's time. It was a mark of the son's respect for his father after their years of strain and it remained a prominent feature of the grounds of the house for over 130 years. When Rose Hill and its grounds were bought by a firm of builders in 1994 a fence was erected and the Watkin memorial, now outside the new boundary, was gradually lost in the encroaching undergrowth of the neighbouring Rose Hill Woods – and forgotten. That is something we will return to.

Chapter 7

The Star

The twenty years from 1860 saw Edward Watkin at the peak of his powers. One magazine article about him in 1879 began: 'Sir Edward is the acknowledged chief of the railway system of the United Kingdom and therefore of the world.' He seemed to be everywhere. One writer said: 'He would pop up in the morning near Shakespeare Cliff near Dover, later in the day head for Manchester, and at night would be found shunted near the Welsh Marches.' His appetite for travel was only matched by his seemingly inexhaustible stamina. Well before his career ended he calculated that he had travelled 1½ million miles by rail. His journeys in Britain were matched by his thirty visits to North America. One American newspaper wrote about him: 'One of the most practical men in England, Sir Edward Watkin, whose reputation is as well-known on this side of the Atlantic as it is in his own country.'

He rarely disappointed journalists looking for a good story. Contemporary descriptions of him include words such as masterful and capricious, talented and vain, sanguine and impetuous, all qualities that made for good copy. The 'judicious lunches' and his trains – through lavish free excursions for people of influence – were part of his publicity machine. He loved to be in the swim of public life, meeting the most famous, being consulted, giving interviews. In the Chetham's Library archives in Manchester are several albums of formal invitations from the most famous people of the age, including royalty.

His many public faces fascinated the Victorians. They never knew what to expect from him. Hamilton Ellis (*British Railway History* (Allen & Unwin, 1954)) calls him an enigma. He was sometimes the Hero, to be cheered, sometimes the Villain, to be booed. In his last years he was the Fool, to be laughed at, though from beyond the grave, as we shall see, he had the last laugh.

In his golden years Watkin was a star. This newspaper article from 1881 is typical of the fascination he exerted on the British public:

Just as the express train is starting for Manchester there is a slight but sufficiently evident awakening on the part of the guard and the railway officials generally. This stir is brought about by the sudden appearance of a grey-haired man with short stubby whiskers. It is none other than Sir Edward Watkin, consulting railway physician and surgeon, and his companion with the cavalry moustache is his intimate friend, Mr Myles Fenton. These chiefs of the rail have awaiting them a saloon carriage, with all appliances for utilising time by the way. Before the train has slipped out of the station, Sir Edward is walking up and down the carriage, with head bent down and hands buried in the pockets of his ulster coat. The habit of marching to and fro while thinking has probably been acquired by Sir Edward Watkin's method of doing correspondence by dictation to a shorthand writer, for it is notorious that he was one of the first to introduce stenography into railway offices. His own explanation is that walking up and down relieves his feelings. Sometimes he sings aloud some not very well-defined hymn of praise. As soon as the train is well under way Sir Edward Watkin and Mr Fenton are seen hard at work together over a despatch box, going through letters. The handsome saloon is an office for the transaction of business. There is great overhauling and note making until, as the sun passes the meridian, a bell has sounded the hour of luncheon. No thoughts of dividends and excursion trains now come between the famous railway doctor and the wing of a chicken.

As the article suggests, Watkin's style of travel on the railways matched his big reputation. He often had his own luxury accommodation, together with a retinue of secretaries and underlings. The last of his private carriages was built in 1890 at a cost of £1,150, the equivalent of over £100,000 today. It had two compartments with walls and ceilings decorated with inlaid woods. The smoke room had two folding tables and four armchairs embellished with the company's monogram. These were complete with hassocks and upholstered in buttoned black leather. A larger compartment contained similar armchairs and a settee, which had tasselled cushions. On the walls were mirrored shelves and framed pictures. At each end of the carriage was a covered balcony decorated with brass work. There was a toilet and an attendant's compartment with a galley for the preparation of meals and refreshments.

What most impressed people who met Watkin was his energy, which was prodigious. One newspaper report referred to 'that general "go" and verve which makes him a phenomenon'. That, and his appetite for travel, meant that he literally lived on trains. Before the plane and the car were invented trains were the fastest and easiest means of getting to business meetings but there must be a suspicion that he secretly enjoyed the astonishment and admiration which his hectic journeyings aroused in people. The Annual General Meetings of his three largest railway companies always took place in the same week even though they were held in different parts of the country. On these occasions Watkin went from London – the Charing Cross Station Hotel was virtually his residence in the capital – to Manchester on the Tuesday afternoon train, stayed in Manchester overnight, chaired the meeting of the MSLR on the Wednesday morning and travelled back to London that afternoon to chair the meetings of the Metropolitan Railway on the Thursday and the SER on the Friday. He would then go back to Rose Hill for the weekend on the 6.15pm train from London. As chairman of all three companies he decided the dates for the meetings.

Where did he get his energy from? He obviously had phenomenal physical resources but – as we saw in his early diary entries – being busy excited and stimulated him. His diary entry for the beginning of October 1847 says: 'I have been busy since the last entry.' (This had been five months earlier.) In fact, during the four summer months the only events he thought worth recording were the places he visited, almost all business trips. September is typical: 1 and 2 Rugby, 3 over Trent, 7 Rugby, 10 over line, 12 over line, 15 Rugby, 16 Atherstone, 18 Rugby, 19 with Polly to Prestwich, 20 Crewe, 21 Leicester, 22 Coventry and Rugby, 23 London, 24 back home with Polly, 25, 26 at home, 27 London, 28 Kettering, Kibworth.

One of Watkin's attractive qualities was that – unlike many ambitious people – he did not try to undermine potential rivals; on the contrary he had a flair for identifying talent. One commentator wrote in 1913: He was always on the look-out for merit among the younger members of his staff. With few exceptions, the foremost railway men of the last quarter of a century were 'Watkin's young men'. He commanded great respect from his managers. Contemporary reports describe his own exceptional talent as a manager, his business acumen and superb negotiating skills.

He was seen as 'strong, striking and masterful' and 'full of courage'. The courage showed itself in the way he tackled problems that others would have turned away from but also in his refusal to admit defeat. One article in an Australian newspaper said: 'If to be irrepressible is the mark of greatness, Sir Edward Watkin is among the greatest personalities of his time.' Even critics said he was a 'doughty buccaneer'. Disraeli called him 'a wary, watchful and aggressive opponent' but awarded him a knighthood. One opponent in Canada referred to Watkin's 'brash but appealing optimism' and the *Railway Times* magazine, not always his friend, wrote: 'It would be impossible for the most severe critic of Sir Edward Watkin not to admire the cheerfulness with which he bears himself under the most adverse circumstances. His pet schemes have lately suffered signal defeat … but nevertheless Sir Edward comes up smiling.' In spite of his pugnacious nature, Watkin never bore a grudge. His greatest opponent in the plan to dig a tunnel under the English Channel was, as we shall see, the formidable Adjutant General Sir (later Lord) Garnet Wolseley. Correspondence between the two men remained friendly throughout the dispute.

Every characteristic about Watkin that so impressed friends and enemies alike: his energy, his refusal to give up (he tried eleven times to get a Channel tunnel bill through Parliament), his eagerness to embark on new schemes, all can be traced back to that compulsion to be top dog which led to his Northenden ninepence. Typical contemporary references were that there was always sure to be some pretty fighting when Sir Edward was involved and revenge, legal battles and animosity were never far. He had always relished a scrap. When Edward and his younger brother were involved in a violent political meeting in Stevenson Square in Manchester Absalom wrote disapprovingly in his diary: 'Several heads were broken in a scuffle. Edward and John took a prominent part.' At another meeting Edward wrote excitedly: 'We mustered in full strength and we had as pretty a row as I ever witnessed. The Chartists were driven out of the hall four times. We regularly thrashed them and passed our own resolutions.' At another meeting it is clear that Edward was responsible for making sure that the main speaker, Richard Cobden, would be heard, without opposition:

Men, handy with their fists, were recruited by Edward Watkin, a future railway magnate, mainly from Irish members of the Manchester

Operatives Anti-Corn Law Association, set up to recruit working-
class converts to the cause.... In cahoots with the police, the organisers
ensured that opponents were kept out of the building.... Those that
did get in ... were roughly handled by the Irish lambs.

But Watkin was no one club golfer. Many opponents made the mistake
of thinking he would always be aggressive, yet he could be suave and
reasonable, as Disraeli's wife saw in Manchester and the committee of
the Marylebone Cricket Club at Lord's would discover. There are many
references to his charm and his thoughtfulness. Once he was showing a
group of men round his new railway bridge over the River Dee. It was a
cold day and he was wearing what a reporter called: 'one of the strangest
pieces of headgear that ever came under my notice'. The report went on:

> It was woven out of coarse grey woollen, with the fluffy side
> outwards, resembling a turban in shape. Sir Edward said it could not
> be blown off, could withstand any reasonable quantity of moisture,
> could be twisted into half-a-dozen different shapes – either forming
> a helmet to protect the neck or a bonnet that was proof against the
> sunshine. It had been specially designed for its owner by an admirer
> in a Lancashire factory, and no duplicate existed. Three months later,
> every member of the party received a facsimile of the original turban,
> with Sir Edward's best wishes for years of useful wear.

Another of his attractive characteristics was his sense of humour. The
newspaper report describing him at work in the train went on: 'While the
engine is taking in fuel there must be no manner of work – it is an interval
for telling stories and cracking jokes. The Chairman of the South Eastern
Railway is famous for his fund of anecdotes, his Lancashire stories.' He
loved speaking to young people, for example at school speech days, which
he always prepared for with carefully chosen illustrations – and stories.
He would often use his ability to tell a good story to deflect criticism in
a meeting when someone raised an awkward question. He would then
move on quickly to something else or even immediately close the meeting
on a happy note. It was only later that people realised the question had
not been answered. One obituary said that opponents would go into a
meeting ready to vote against him but when they came out at the end
they said they had supported him but could not remember why they
had changed their mind. He was at his best in meetings. ('Decisive and

business-like with unfailing good humour'). Nimble Ned was a master of figures. One report said: 'We listened to him with interest speaking figures extempore for an hour together'.

This is from a newspaper report of a public meeting with voters in Stockport when he was their local MP:

> We remember him bringing down the house in a rather noisy meeting among his old constituents by throwing off his coat, the more thoroughly to show his identification with an audience of working men. The neat, dapper little figure stands erect and full displayed, the fingers straightening down the spotless and unwrinkled waistcoat. Keen, watchful face, roving, inquisitive eye. An interruption is his opportunity – he has a facility of getting on the right side.

Watkin was described by *The Times* newspaper as: 'unquestionably known to the public at large better than any railway man in the country'. Yet, as we have seen from his own descriptions of his mental state, he shared with his father a tendency towards depression and lack of confidence that was a complete contrast to the public figure. This perhaps explains the curious fact that though he lived in an age when the camera was beginning to record everyday life, he seems to have been surprisingly camera-shy. There are remarkably few photographs of him. When he entertained Gladstone and Lloyd George to dinner at his chalet in north Wales after the opening of a new path up Snowdon he is missing from the group photo taken in front of his chalet. (Perhaps he had taken umbrage that his guest, Gladstone, failed to mention in his speech at the opening the reason for the occasion or the man who had brought it about but instead spoke at length on Welsh land reform.) When the first sod of earth was turned by the Countess of Wharncliffe to start the building of the Great Central Railway, the creation of which was entirely down to him, he presented the ceremonial spade to her but is missing from the photograph of the ceremony. There is only one photo of him with his family.

Even during his years of stardom he guarded his privacy. But he was soon to discover that fame is lived out on the edge of a cliff with spectacular views but with the danger of a fall always lurking. The love that the public shower onto their favourite stars is only matched by their delight when things go wrong. Watkin had come big. That was to make his fall all the greater.

Chapter 8

The Lost Channel Tunnel

Watkin's achievements in Canada and the knighthood that followed from a grateful British government left him full of confidence in his own powers. Too full. On his return to the UK in 1869 his mood echoed that diary entry as a young man: 'Nothing, no difficulty is too strong for the power I have at my disposal.' A veteran journalist, John Boon, recorded that he dined with Watkin on the night he returned from Canada: 'On the night of the dinner he told me of a wonderful scheme by which Esquimalt (a settlement in the south of Vancouver Island) could be linked up with Liverpool and through his systems to the Continent and the Baghdad Railway. India, also, was to be brought into contact.'

Five years after he returned to Britain he embarked on a project that was to dominate his thoughts for the next twenty years: the construction of a railway tunnel from the South Coast of England to France. It was an idea big enough for British North America but he had returned to a small island and authorities with minds to match and it proved in the end to be his greatest failure. His repeated attempts to get the scheme through Parliament were to earn him public ridicule and another nickname: 'The Bore of the Channel Tunnel'.

The idea of joining England to France was actually first voiced by the Roman Emperor Caligula in the first century AD. His plan was to tie boats together coast to coast. In more recent times a proposal for a tunnel in 1802 was to use horse-drawn carriages on a road. That idea had got off to a bad start in Britain since it had been suggested by a man who was never the most popular Frenchman in British governing circles: Napoleon Bonaparte. Prior to Watkin's appearance on the scene every initiative had come from the French side, so it was perhaps not surprising that his enthusiasm was greeted with delight by the French. The European Peace League in Paris had been excited that the tunnel under the Channel would, together with the Suez Canal and the St Gotthard rail tunnel, bring 'peace to the world'. An imaginative portrait published by the League depicted classically dressed figures (all female) in an open-air chariot pulled by a steam locomotive, the first train from London to Marseille.

The suggestion of a Channel tunnel was, however, received more coolly in Britain. Even though it had conquered half the world through its Empire, Britain was at heart still an island, the original NIMBY (Not In My Back Yard). A famous newspaper placard read: 'Fog in the Channel. Continent cut off.' Apart from those territories where the British had re-created the Mother Country, 'Abroad' was something to be viewed with suspicion since it was full of foreigners and everyone knew that foreigners were not to be trusted. Those parts of France round Calais which had remained part of England until 1558 had been subject to English law and order. The area was known as the Pale. Outside, where foreigners lived, was 'beyond the Pale', a phrase that is still a synonym for 'beyond the boundaries of acceptable behaviour'.

As long as a Channel tunnel was just an idea to talk about, it could be tolerated in Britain. But the coming of the trains meant that it only needed a man with vision and determination for the idea to be changed into a serious proposition. That man was Edward Watkin, bursting with confidence on his return from Canada.

By 1880 he was the chairman or director of railway companies leading from London to the South Coast of England and from the French coast to Paris. All that was preventing his great plan to link the two capital cities by rail from becoming reality was 22 miles under the English Channel, and Parliament – presumably not realising his determination – had given him permission to start digging an experimental tunnel.

Watkin plunged into the scheme with his usual relish. His Channel tunnel would be the longest tunnel in the world, a bonus for a man who loved to come first. He had earlier met a number of promoters in France who had expressed interest in his tunnel, one of them the contractor for the Suez Canal. He commissioned an analysis of the weather in the Channel, which revealed that there had been only ninety calm days in the previous twelve months. A half-hour journey in a train instead of a wretched journey by boat over one of the most turbulent stretches of water in the world was highly attractive. In the past even Queen Victoria had said that the women of Britain would be grateful for a tunnel, if only to avoid being seasick on their way to France. She had been much influenced in her view by her beloved Prince Albert, who was in favour of a tunnel. But by the time Watkin began his campaign in 1880 Albert had been dead for almost twenty years and the queen was now opposed to the tunnel. She told Disraeli that the idea was 'very objectionable'.

Watkin's preparations were impressive. He chose a site at Shakespeare Cliff, halfway between Dover and Folkestone (coincidentally in the constituency for which he was now the Member of Parliament) and had the 22 miles under the Channel surveyed by Professor Sir William Boyd Dawkins, the pre-eminent geologist of the day. (Dawkins' tunnel survey also revealed rich deposits of coal, which became, after Watkin's death, the lucrative Kent coalfield.) Dawkins wrote later: 'To Sir Edward is due the credit of translating geological theory into ascertained fact.' He confirmed that a 300ft thick seam of chalk and clay extended the whole length under the sea, that it would not leak and that it would be easy to drill. The stratum was 'very like hard cheese' and the atmosphere in the tunnel would be 'very much purer than that of most drawing rooms'. The Channel turned out to be 'an extremely shallow puddle with a maximum depth of 200 feet'. Half of it was less than 100ft deep, hence the turbulence of the waters. Watkin also gained spiritual support from the Archbishop of Canterbury, who wrote, 'Providence has placed that wonderful material between the coasts of England and France with a view to ultimate communication.'

Watkin bought a newly invented drilling machine, which would also ventilate the shaft as it went along since it was powered by compressed air. The French started to dig a tunnel from their side of the Channel, at first using explosives and manual labour but they were so impressed by Watkin's methods that they soon bought one of his machines. The plan was to construct twin tunnels for ventilation purposes and for security in the event of an accident in one. (In 1988 Eurotunnel adopted both Watkin's twin-tunnel scheme and his site.)

Digging began in October 1880 and made good progress at a rate of 200ft a week. Watkin estimated that the first boring would be finished within five years. When concern was expressed that the smoke from the trains might suffocate passengers in the tunnel, Watkin borrowed his solution from an earlier tunnel enthusiast in 1802. Albert Mathieu had wanted to build an island on the Varne Sandbank halfway across the Channel, which is only 10ft below the surface of the water at low tide and even at high tide is only 30ft down. Mathieu's idea was that the island would be where coaches could change their horses. Watkin's plan was typically bold – he would build a commercial port on it with a ventilation shaft down into his tunnel.

The formidable public relations machine of the 'master of the judicious lunch' swung into action. The Prince of Wales (the future Edward VII) and the Princess, the Lord Mayor of London, the Archbishop of Canterbury and the prime minister, Gladstone, all made the journey from London to Shakespeare Cliff. Going to view the tunnel became for a time part of the fashionable London Scene. Watkin arranged free passes from Charing Cross Station and champagne receptions in the cavern-like entrance, which was well-ventilated, lit by electricity and decorated with potted palms. The ladies were delighted to find that their dresses were as clean at the end of their visit as they had been at the beginning. Sir Edward often travelled with the men down to the tunnel in the standard bucket from the surface then in carriages pushed by hand to the tunnel face. One journalist wrote after his visit:

> A glass of sherry and a biscuit compensated us for the fatigue of our under-the-sea trip and after signing our names in the book we entrained and proceeded to Dover, and ere long were seated round a well and handsomely furnished table in the dining room of the Lord Warden Hotel. After doing justice to an excellent lunch, several toasts were proposed, that of 'The Queen' of course taking the lead.

But storm clouds were gathering. Influential politicians in the Tory party, senior civil servants, generals, dukes and *The Times* newspaper were becoming alarmed at Watkin's plans. His tunnel was forging ahead and the dastardly 'Frogs', with a tunnel of their own from near Calais, were planning to meet Watkin's tunnel halfway across. The opposition began to crystallise into a single fear: invasion. The fact that the last war with France had been sixty-seven years ago and the French were in no condition to start a war (they had been occupied and defeated by the Germans only nine years previously and were still paying reparations) counted for nothing.

In the 1880s the British Empire was the most powerful force in the world, so spread out that the sun literally never set on it. Britannia ruled the waves – and not just the waves of the world's great oceans. The French and the Germans call the Channel la Manche and der Ärmel. Both words mean 'The Sleeve' but the British knew who the <u>English</u> Channel really belonged to. In a phrase he must have regretted when he later decided to support Watkin, Gladstone called it the 'silver streak' and the 22 miles of water between England and France began to take on an almost religious significance. One general wrote in a letter to *The Times*: 'Providence has given us the sea as a safeguard', thus preserving divine neutrality after the Archbishop's intervention on Watkin's side.

Sir Edward was coming up against a curious fault line in the way many British people saw themselves: strong enough to invade and conquer every continent in the world but almost paranoid about invasion by foreigners. It is a paradox that has lasted into the twenty-first century. A letter in a national newspaper in June 2015 expressed fear at the number of immigrants trying to get into Britain and concluded: 'Please close the Channel Tunnel and return the UK to an island nation'. In the 1880s the question was: What if the French or the newly united Germans attacked in their thousands through Watkin's tunnel, captured Dover and marched on London? Charles Dickens said that the Royal Navy would look on as a helpless spectator while the French simply walked underneath their ships to 'take their revenge for Waterloo'. The press fanned the flames and among popular book titles of 1882 were *The capture of the Channel Tunnel* and *How John Bull lost London*. An article in the *Railway News* reported:

> Some of the leading agitators among the working men in this country, under the auspices of Sir E. Watkin, have been despatched to France to act in concert with the anarchists and the dynamite fraternity. The ruffianism of Paris and Lyons look forward hopefully to the time when they will be enabled to extend their benevolent schemes of rapine, plunder and bloodshed to this country. They want the French to come in their millions.

The *Spectator* magazine warned that Irish Republicans, in league with the French, might rush the tunnel, and the *Nineteenth Century* magazine suggested that the French might 'carry distinguished English people on the engine as hostages'. Cardinal Newman forecast gloomily: 'Satan is unloosed in France and England's turn is next.' A series of editorials in *The Times* thundered. The President of the Royal Academy added his view that 'the Tunnel would be in bad taste'. A cartoon in the famous satirical magazine *Punch*, showing Watkin as the 'Spider' and Gladstone, the prime minister, as the 'Fly', was among the more restrained reactions.

All through the arguments about a Channel tunnel the French looked on bemused. But French enthusiasm for the tunnel only increased the Establishment's suspicions, particularly when it was shared by Germany, Great Britain's rival at the end of the 1800s, flexing its muscles after winning the Franco-Prussian War ten years before and becoming a single nation. An article in a German magazine at the time commented:

> What a strange nation the English are! They fought off invasion by Philip II of Spain and Napoleon Bonaparte but are terrified at the prospect that a few French soldiers disguised as tourists and hiding their guns in their bags will make off with London in their suitcases. Let us hope that we shall see the day when real patriotism will be united with a cosmopolitan view of the world so that we will be able to travel from Scotland to East India or at least from London to Constantinople in a railway carriage.

The insularity of the British Establishment had been shown many years earlier by the prime minister, Lord Palmerston, when he said to the pro-tunnel Prince Albert: 'You would think very differently if you had been born in this island. The object of a tunnel would be to shorten a distance we find already too short.'

The most effective opposition of all came from Lord Wolseley. He had fought in Burma and India and the Crimea (where he lost an eye in battle) and was the most respected soldier in the British Army, although Gilbert and Sullivan were widely thought to have had him in mind when they wrote the wonderfully absurd: 'I am the model of a modern Major-General' for their comic opera *The Pirates of Penzance*. His evidence before the parliamentary inquiry into Watkin's scheme was frightening at the time, even if parts of it read now like Corporal Jones in Dad's Army: 'Don't panic! Don't panic!' He stated:

> Seizure on this side might be carried out by a force of 2000 men any night, who could suddenly pounce upon the approaches on this side. The sentry and the sleepy sergeant might be easily disposed of and the few men on guard could be made prisoners whilst asleep on their guard bed. In four or five hours afterwards 2000 men could be sent through the tunnel to their support, and before daybreak the tunnel would have completely passed into the enemy's possession. Before morning dawned Dover might easily be in possession of 20000 of the

enemy, and every succeeding hour would add to that number. Once the enemy force, now swelled to 150000 men, had reached London and occupied the Thames from there to the arsenal at Woolwich, it could dictate its own terms of peace, estimated at a rough guess as the payment of six million pounds and the surrender of the British Fleet, with the English end of the tunnel remaining permanently in the hands of the French so that the perpetual yoke of servitude would be ours for ever. England would cease to exist as a nation.

In later evidence he said that the initial 2,000 invaders 'would evade all suspicion by being dressed as ordinary passengers' and that they would arrive in 20 trains at 12-minute intervals. He did not explain how nobody in England would notice them coming or wonder at 2,000 young Frenchmen all carrying rifles and single tickets to Dover, with their weapons hidden under their ordinary coats and clanking. Or how the French would be able to commandeer twenty trains over a period of 4 hours without anyone in England becoming alarmed.

Watkin said Wolseley's evidence was based on 'hobgoblin arguments', which was pretty restrained in the circumstances. He said that a hostile army could be seen off by a few old women armed with broomsticks. He reminded people of similar opposition in the 1840s to the building of a railway line from Southampton to London. One horrified colonel at that time had written that it would be 'a tempting invitation to an enemy's fleet for the occupation of the Solent and Southampton Water' and that this would lead to the invasion of London. Watkin said that it would be a simple matter to lay explosives, which in an emergency could blow up the tunnel entrance or flood it, simply by pressing a button on his desk. As late as 1907 one newspaper cartoon had an answer even if the tunnel was flooded: it showed a platoon of foreign soldiers marching towards Britain with bayonets fixed and all wearing diving suits.

The idea of destroying the tunnel in an emergency took on a life of its own. When the idea of a Channel tunnel was revived just before the First World War it was widely believed that there would be an Ivory Button controlled by an officer of the Horse Guards in London. There was great concern about the strain – as with the nuclear option later in the twentieth century – which would be put on the officer who had to decide when to press the button. There was less concern about the passengers on the other trains in the tunnel as it was being blown up.

A letter to *The Times* in June 1881 tried to set out a reasoned answer to Sir Garnet:

There may be danger from the Channel Tunnel to the navvies who construct it, to the travellers who use it, and to the Companies who pay for it; but none whatsoever, I will be bound, to the good people of Kent, or the other loyal subjects of the Queen. Consider the position (of the tunnel). The opening to it on this side must be some distance inland, in order to obtain a proper gradient. It must be within a short distance of Dover, where there is a garrison, and of Shorecliffe, where there is a camp. Within three hours' notice of any alarm, several thousand troops of all arms from London, Woolwich and Portsmouth could be on the spot. Unless every telegraph clerk, every railway servant, every soldier at Dover were asleep or drugged, an inroad might be stopped, as Sir Edward Watkin suggests, by a pound of dynamite or a keg of gunpowder. It is quite certain that a couple of small forts near the mouth of the tunnel would render any such enterprise, whether by sea or tunnel, absolutely impossible. As a practical matter, it appears to me that the only question which either the promoters of the tunnel or the public need to ask is, 'Will it pay?' not 'Will the French invade?'

Colonel Beaumont, who always claimed to have invented the compressed-air drilling machine, tried to calm the hysteria which was gripping the ranks of the Establishment. Faced with the prospect of thousands of Frenchmen coming secretly through the tunnel he said: 'They cannot come by train as irrespective of any suspicions by the booking clerks special train arrangements would have to be made to carry so large a number. They cannot march as they would be run over by the trains running as they would do at intervals of ten minutes or oftener without cessation day and night.'

Watkin too tried to deal with the hobgoblin arguments rationally. *The Times* letter writer had pointed out that the train would have to emerge gradually up a gradient before exiting the tunnel mouth, Watkin, speaking in a parliamentary debate, described the tunnel entrance as 'a frontier no bigger than the door of the House of Commons'. (Field Marshal Moltke said: 'You might as well talk of invading (England) through the door of my library.') In a speech in 1888 Watkin made another suggestion designed to allay fears: 'It is proposed to lift trains by hydraulic machinery from the level of the tunnel to the surface, where they could join the main line. The notion of pouring thousands of men into the Tunnel from the Continental end falls to the ground.' To overcome the fear that the Royal Navy would be helpless if trains were out of sight a simple device was suggested for the trains leaving France. Instead of disappearing underground at the French side of the Channel the train would travel a short distance out on a viaduct over the sea in the open air then double back before going underground en route for England. The viaduct would be a kind of fuse, easily blown up by the Royal Navy like a bridge, if invasion was threatened. This proposal was actually put forward by the French.

Numerous ideas were suggested that would defend the tunnel from the French invaders. Wolseley met each with essentially the same argument: What if it didn't work? These were his responses as recorded at the official hearings into the tunnel scheme:

- A hundred riflemen at the Dover end could defend a tunnel. 'What if they relaxed?'
- A series of defensive devices could be installed. 'Accidents happen.'
- How about electrically operated mines? 'The gunpowder might be damp.'
- The tunnel could be flooded with sea-water. 'The water conduits might become choked and the drains might be rendered useless by treachery.'

He ended his evidence: 'Surely John Bull will not endanger his birth-right, his property, in fact all that man can hold most dear ... simply in order that men and women may cross between England and France without running the risk of being seasick'.

What was missing in attempts to counteract the what now seem absurd statements of Sir Garnet Wolseley was the characteristic which is still seen by many European countries as specially English – an irreverent sense of humour. But Wolseley was too respected to be laughed at. His name had entered the English language: 'All Sir Garnet' was a common expression for 'All correct'. Mocking him would have caused a backlash.

The idea that the French could invade England through a hole in the ground took root and a mood not far short of paranoia set in. It was noted by the government that the tunnel supporters 'seem to be chiefly foreign marshals and generals'. A mob smashed the windows of Watkin's Channel tunnel company in Westminster and the government ordered him to stop digging. The British company and its French equivalent had completed in all 3.6 miles of the 22 before tunnelling ceased. Watkin tried again and again to get Parliament to support his Channel tunnel and even proposed a treaty to be signed by the Great Powers to guarantee the neutrality of the tunnel. But his efforts in the early 1880s really marked the end of any Channel tunnel scheme for a hundred years. A letter to Gladstone in July 1883 showed his exasperation: 'The French will go beyond halfway towards England. What will you do then? Declare war?' (In the end, the French abandoned their efforts after a High Court ruling.) Another letter, in May 1890, describes the attitude of the tunnel opponents as 'dog-in-the-manger'.

Why did Watkin's scheme fail? One American newspaper summed up the main public argument against it:

> Sir Edwin [*sic*] Watkin tells us that the French are very eager to have the tunnel proceeded with and that they have finished their 2200 yards in admirable style. That is the very point. The reasons which render the French so desirous for the tunnel are precisely those which make Englishmen fight shy of it. The silver streak is their protection and they have built an enormous fleet chiefly to enable them to hold command over it. Now it is to be placed at the disposal of an enemy.

There was also an economic reason behind the opposition to the tunnel, though this was not voiced in public. The project coincided with a period of cuts in British Army and Royal Navy spending. It was in the interests of those who opposed the cuts to emphasise the danger of invasion.

There was another more personal reason for Watkin's failure: the methods he had so often used successfully to get his own way in the railway world – a mixture of charm and aggression. His great successes had always been achieved by the force of his dominant personality, but this is not the attribute of a team player and in this biggest of games he needed supporters. The pragmatic tone of his speeches in Parliament, sometimes liberal, sometimes conservative, had alienated many of his earlier friends and eroded his power base. He was never a political party loyalist. His tried and trusted methods were inadequate against opponents who were used to victories at the highest level and were not fazed by threats. One writer's view was that 'Edward Watkin ... lost his battle with the inner circles of London society'. But the crucial factor was that Watkin had spectacularly failed to judge the national mood. One commentator has written of the Victorians' 'yearning for stability, some safe and sure anchorage within a frighteningly fast-changing world'. In spite of their Empire the British were at heart still an island folk, in some respects almost parochial, whereas Watkin, as he had shown in Canada, was a visionary with his eyes on new and exciting horizons. The British people sided with the government.

After Watkin's death there were many more attempts to introduce a Channel tunnel bill. One was in 1913, just before the opening of the First World War. In August of that year a column in the *Observer* newspaper contained an appreciation of Edward Watkin. It was written by 'Cross Bencher', the pen-name of Henry Lucy, the first ever parliamentary lobby correspondent and one of the most famous English political journalists of the day. In his article Lucy describes the antagonism in 1880 between Watkin and Joseph Chamberlain MP, the President of the Board of Trade, over the issue of a Channel tunnel. Chamberlain had set up a Departmental Committee to inquire into a tunnel's feasibility. Until it reported back, he ordered all work on Watkin's tunnel to be halted.

> Sir Edward Watkin was furious. He was not averse to fighting but he had no option against obedience to the command. He comforted himself by cherishing a pleasing proposal. He confided to me that in the event of the Tunnel works being permanently stopped he would erect on the site a column of stone lofty enough to be seen by all vessels passing up and down the Channel, visible on a clear day from the coast of responsive France. From half a sheet of notepaper drawn from his waistcoat pocket he read the proposed inscription. It set forth how the opening of the Tunnel had been visited by the Prince of Wales and other Royal Personages, by Mr Gladstone [at the time prime minister], by the Speaker of the House of Commons and by a considerable contingent of peers and commoners; and how, when all seemed prosperous and all the world applauded, the works were peremptorily stopped 'by Joseph Chamberlain of Birmingham'.

The article concludes: 'It is evident that before long the House of Commons will again be consulted on the matter. Should the campaign eventually prove successful, it must not be forgotten that "the onlie begetter" was Edward Watkin.'

An evocative photograph of a tunnel inspection in 1916 shows the structure of the 1880 tunnel was still sound. In 1919 the Cabinet, led by the prime minister, Lloyd George, approved the plan but were defeated by a combination of the military top brass and the Secretary to the Cabinet, who refused to include their decision in the Cabinet minutes.

One leading advocate of a tunnel in the 1924–9 government was Winston Churchill, who ridiculed fears of invasion through what he called a 'tiny tube'. In 1929, however, the Earl of Crawford warned that practices that were common among foreigners – homosexuality, pornography and drug trafficking – would spread to Britain if a tunnel was dug. The proposal that followed his evidence was defeated in the Commons by only seven votes (Winston Churchill voted in favour). Just before the Second World War Churchill declared: 'There are few projects against which there exists a deeper and more enduring prejudice than the construction of a railway tunnel between Dover and Calais'. In 1944 there was a brief renewal of interest in the tunnel, when Wolseley's ghost rattled its chains. The Germans were reported to be digging at the site of the 1880 tunnel. In fact, they were building launching pads for their V2 rockets. In 1949 a Foreign Office memorandum warned that a tunnel project would undermine 'that unquestioning sense of superiority which forms an essential element in British self-confidence'. In 1973 the Chiefs of Defence Staff only abandoned their suggestion to put a nuclear bomb in the tunnel in case of invasion when it was pointed out that the tunnel would in effect become the barrel of a gun and destroy parts of Kent. In the early 1980s during short-lived renewed interest an executive of the shipping line P&O expressed his company's understandable opposition to a tunnel in a striking sentence: 'A lot of water has to pass under the bridge before the Channel Tunnel gets off the ground.'

And that was that until July 1986, when Mrs Thatcher agreed with the French President, François Mitterrand, that a joint, private project should be approved. (In an echo of the man who first had the idea of joining France to England almost 2,000 years earlier the French President said that Mrs Thatcher had the eyes of Caligula and added that she also had the mouth of Marilyn Monroe.)

In spite of continuing opposition (the top women's magazine *Woman's Own* described the French as a nation of pretty and petty crooks), digging started in 1988. At one point the drilling machine broke through into Watkin's tunnel, abandoned over a century earlier. It was dry. Watkin had had the technology for Britain and France to have a Channel tunnel in the late nineteenth century. But the government had had the power to say no. In an interesting reversal of the government's fears in 1882, Mrs Thatcher saw the tunnel as a means of extending Britain's influence, though like everyone else her own planning experts wildly over-estimated the tunnel's popularity. Forecasts of passenger numbers for the first year varied from 17 million to 48 million. The actual figure in 2003 was 6.3 million. According to Professor Wray, the closest estimate of 4.5 million had been made 121 years earlier – by Edward Watkin.

Some months before the opening, an event tinged with irony occurred. The ventilation shafts of the Woodhead Tunnel on the line between Manchester and Sheffield (one of the Wonders of the World when it was opened in 1845) were sealed off and trains were run through to replicate the atmosphere in the coming Channel Tunnel. The tunnel in the Pennines had been part of Watkin's main line from Manchester to London, then Paris. It had been closed twenty years earlier.

On 6 May 1994 the Channel Tunnel was officially opened by the Queen and the President of France. The powers-that-be threw the Watkin family a sop when Edward's great-granddaughter, Dorothea Worsley-Taylor, was invited to the ceremony, to be presented with a bronze medal to mark the occasion. It was a nice gesture and showed somebody had been reading their history books. But Sir Edward would have pointed out that bronze medals are not for winners.

No trace remains now of the entrance to Watkin's tunnel near to the present tunnel. Where the future King Edward VII and every other notable person in Victorian Britain came to see Watkin's Wonder is now a beautiful country park, Samphire Hoe, created by using 4.9 million cubic metres of chalk marl from the excavations of the present Channel Tunnel. 'Hoe' means 'a piece of land jutting out into the sea' and Samphire Hoe has increased the size of the UK by 90 acres. In 1890 Watkin had promised that his tunnel would 'extend the British Empire some ten or twelve miles in the direction of France'.

Absalom Watkin (1787–1861).

Edward Watkin (1819–1901).

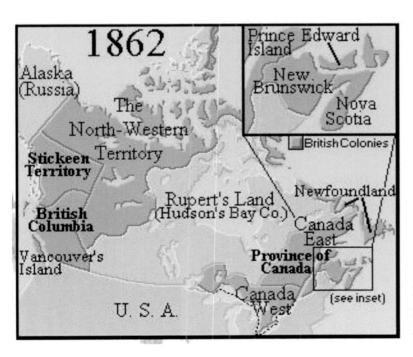

Map of British North America before the Dominion of Canada was created.

Portrait of Edward Watkin – on the paper in his hand is written 'Canada'.

The last photograph of Absalom Watkin – at Rose Hill, with his wife and Edward's two children. (*Chetham's Library, Manchester*)

The only surviving photo of Edward Watkin with his family. (*Chetham's Library, Manchester*)

Watkin's 1880 Channel tunnel, open for inspection in 1916.

The entrance to Watkin's 1880 Channel tunnel in 1984 – now sealed off. (*Subterranea Britannica*)

Rural Wembley and 'Watkin's Folly' in the 1890s.

The sad end of the Great Tower in London.

The Wembley Tower that never was and the current stadium. (*M. Paterson/London Historians*)

The defence of Lord's cricket ground against Watkin's railway. (Punch *magazine*)

Lanchester Lodge with a Lanchester car on the driveway and Sir Alfred Watkin (left). (*Gwynedd Record Office*)

Watkin's daughter, Harriette. (*Chetham's Library, Manchester*)

Edward Watkin – the final photograph. (*The Watkin Collection, Chetham's Library, Manchester*)

Aerial view of the Watkin estate in 1929. (*P. Higginbotham*)

The 'forlorn ruin' of Rose Hill in the late 1990s. (*Manchester Evening News*)

Rose Hill House today. (*Author*)

£50 REWARD

Some Member of the Committee of MAJOR SEDDON having circulated a

FALSE AND SCANDALOUS
ATTACK

Upon me in reference to HUDSON'S BAY, I hereby offer the above Reward to any one who will give the Name and Address of the offending Committee-man; and I have to state that Major Seddon's Senior Partner, RICHARD POTTER, Esq., of the firm of PRICE, POTTER, WALKER & Co., is the only person who can explain the transaction in question, so unjustly described, as he, and he alone, had the sole control of the financial arrangements impugned. I add that the man NELSON, whose name is used, IS A RASCAL, he having obtained £100 from me some years ago for expenses of a journey in America which he never performed.

EDW. W. WATKIN.

Royal Hotel, Grimsby,
July 31st, 1877.

Scandal in Grimsby – the 1877 by-election. (*Grimsby Library*)

The Icebergs – the Mona Lisa of the Dallas Museum of Art, Texas. (*S. Canterbury*)

Under the waters of the English Channel what remains of the 1880 tunnel has an interesting relic as a companion. After the drilling machine had finished its work in December 1990 it could not reverse since the tunnel behind it had been lined with concrete and was now too narrow. The machine steered off to one side, bored a short tunnel as its own grave and was abandoned. It is still down there.

The entrance to Watkin's trial boring of 1880, a few hundred feet further along the shoreline from his original tunnel and next to the present tunnel at Shakespeare Cliff near Dover, was accessible until the late 1990s but is now sealed with a steel plate. Carved in the rock wall 150ft in by one of the miners is the only memorial to Watkin's lost Channel tunnel: 'THIS TUNNEL WAS BEGUBNUGN [*sic*] IN 1880 WILLIAM SHARP'. But there is nobody there to read it, a sad final verdict on a great enterprise that would have shaped the development of Europe in the twentieth century.

Chapter 9

An Eiffel Tower in London

His failure to gain parliamentary approval for his Channel tunnel seriously damaged the reputation of Nimble Ned, the supreme fixer. Someone who had seemed so confident, always pulling off dazzling deals then moving on to another amazing plan, had made many fair-weather friends. As the sun went in, those friends began to disappear but not his enemies, mainly lesser mortals, eager to dance on the grave of his public reputation. After the courts had put a stop to the Channel tunnel project what became known as 'Watkin's Folly' made them even happier.

The centrepiece of the Paris Exhibition of 1889 was a 984ft (324m) high tower, designed by Gustav Eiffel. The tallest man-made structure in the world had for the past 3,800 years been the Great Pyramid at Giza, 455ft (139m), although a few years before the Eiffel Tower was built the cathedrals of Hamburg, Rouen and Cologne, and finally the Washington Monument had topped the pyramid by a few feet. But Gustav Eiffel's sensational tower was over 400ft higher than even the Washington Monument. It had originally been planned as a temporary structure built just for the Exhibition but within a few months of its opening it had paid for itself with thousands of customers returning again and again to see the amazing views over Paris. It became a symbol of the capital of France and still is.

Watkin was fascinated by the tower and in July 1889 he suggested to his friend Gladstone that they and their families should visit the Paris Exhibition. On 3 September they set off together. The Exhibition was certainly worth a visit (though to the English not a patch on their Great Exhibition at the Crystal Palace nearly half a century earlier) but for Watkin it was in reality just a sideshow. He had already decided to build a tower in London and had registered a new company, the Metropolitan Tower Construction Company, three weeks earlier. The real purpose of his visit to Paris was to see the French rival. Gladstone, who had no head for heights, could not make it to the top of the tower but of course Watkin did, and fired with enthusiasm he arranged to meet M. Eiffel to try to persuade him to build an Eiffel Tower in London. Eiffel declined. He said that the French might feel he was 'not as good a Frenchman as I hope I am', a patriotic statement somewhat weakened by an offer he made later to build another tower in Chicago. Two other considerations in his decision might have been uncertainty about funding (the Eiffel Tower had been part-financed by the French government whereas the Wembley Tower was going to depend solely on private money) and Watkin's only requirement: his tower had to be bigger than the one in Paris.

At first Watkin had thought of building his tower opposite King's Cross Station but that would mean the railway revenue generated by customers would have put money in the pockets of the directors of the Great Northern Railway, whose trains ran into King's Cross. Anyway, by the early 1890s his plans had grown and needed more space than central London could provide. The tower, apart from becoming the London landmark, was now to be the centrepiece of a great landscaped pleasure park with sports fields and entertainments for the masses. It was a typically grand Watkin concept, perhaps a defiant gesture to the small minds that had so far blocked his tunnel under the English Channel.

The site he finally chose was a gamble, 9 miles from central London in a rural corner of Middlesex. The sheep outnumbered the people and local trains stopped for a 'church interval' between 11am and noon on Sundays so that their crews could attend divine service. The closest village had a population of just over 200 but its name was destined to become famous throughout the world: Wembley. (In Anglo-Saxon times its name had echoes of the football chant: 'Wemba Lea'.) The most notable feature of the area was the beautiful 289 acres of the Wembley Park Estate, owned by the Revd John Grey and created in the eighteen century by Humphrey Repton, who designed the gardens of Woburn Abbey and Longleat and first coined the phrase 'landscape gardener'. Revd Gray was willing to sell and the site was right next to one of Watkin's lines. There was a river which could be dammed to form an ornamental lake, even a hill 170ft above sea level at the south end of the park, on which his tower could be built. He wrote to a friend: 'Although the atmosphere of London may not be so favourable to extensive views as Paris, the view would be incomparably superior.'

The deal was soon done and by early in 1890 the estate had been bought by Watkin's Metropolitan Railway for £32,929 18s. 7d. (£3 million in today's money). A new station was built at a cost of £7,722 0s. 10d. and named Wembley Park. (Strangely, the excavations for the station dug up the jaw of a hippopotamus containing several perfect teeth, and the tusks of an elephant.) No photographs of the original station have survived but a drawing shows that it had two platforms and a booking office, though no shelter against the weather. While the park was being constructed the station was open only on Saturday afternoons to cater for the matches of the nearby Old Westminster Football Club, though later through-tickets to Wembley Park were available from all the stations of the MSLR, SER and Metropolitan Railway, the three major companies that Watkin controlled. By spring 1894 the lake, complete with an artificial waterfall, was ready, there was a cricket pitch, a racecourse, a variety hall, a bandstand and – putting a marker down for sporting history – a football pitch.

Wembley Park opened for business on 12 May 1894. Two days later another tower was opened 170 miles further north. It had been built by the same company that was constructing Watkin's 'Tower in London' and it too was modelled on the tower in Paris. Ironically, Blackpool Tower quickly gained the iconic status that the tower in London was never to achieve.

For Watkin the great showman, the Wembley opening was a strangely tentative affair, lacking his usual buzz. It was almost as if he sensed failure. In a report to his fellow directors he had said that the project should operate at first on 'an experimental basis'. Extraordinarily, initially it was closed at weekends so missed out on the days when the customers were most likely to come. It had been intended that the tower would be completed for the grand opening day of the park, but it was nowhere near ready.

Nonetheless, in spite of its low-key opening, the park 'in the middle of nowhere' was an immediate success and Londoners in their thousands made the journey on Watkin's railway from the Smoke, as London was called in those days, to breathe clean air and enjoy the wide open spaces, the lake and its waterfall and water chute, the beautiful plants and trees (many parts of London were bare of trees), and the marvellous views. A poster from 1894 advertises an 'Athletic and Cycle Meeting', organised by the Metropolitan Railway Mutual Provident Society, with additional attractions that include Grotesque Boxing on a raft on the lake, Monster Balloon Ascent and Parachute Descent, a Magnificent Display of Fireworks and a Grand Water Show conducted by Professor H.R. Pearce. In its first full season Wembley Park attracted more than 120,000 customers and right up to the outbreak of war in 1914 it was a popular picnic spot for families. Part of it was leased out to local farmers for grazing their sheep, for stacking hay and as somewhere to keep their horses. One farmer is recorded as leasing a field and a rickyard just before the outbreak of the First World War and a wonderfully nostalgic photograph shows another farmer letting his horse through a gate. In the rural distance of the image can be seen the base of Watkin's tower.

That was the problem – the tower was only ever a base. Its planning stage had been ambitious and exciting. It was going to make a tremendous impact and not just in London. It would be the tallest man-made structure in history, 1,200ft high (big enough to put the French in their place, with ninepence to spare) and, being visible from all over London, in Watkin's words, 'its own advertisement'. Watkin launched an international competition with prizes of 500 and 250 guineas (the equivalent of £50,000 and £25,000). The sixty-eight entries that were submitted came from the United States, Canada, France, Italy, Sweden and Turkey, as well as from the UK, though it is noticeable that the best British architects and design companies did not bid for the contract. Perhaps there were doubts about the credibility of the scheme – and its financing – and those with the highest reputation did not want to take a risk.

Most of the entries were bizarre. One design, made up of a Tower of Pisa, not leaning but resting on a plinth modelled on the Albert Memorial in Kensington Gardens, was 2,296ft high. Another resembled a spiralled wedding cake and was to be ascended for its first 1,000ft by train. Another would carry passengers up on mules and provided for them to descend by 'captive parachute', four at a time. The selling point of one was that it would extract pure air from 1,000ft up and feed it into houses below 'through pipes like gas'. Another had a siren foghorn and a phonograph to advertise products to the customers in the park – and presumably to the neighbours for miles around. Perhaps the strangest was based on the Great Pyramid at Giza. It was designed to be inhabited by vegetarians, who would grow their own food in hanging gardens in the sky. Finally, there was one design magnificent only in its name: 'The Muniment of

Hieroglyphics Emblematical of British History During Queen Victoria's Reign Tower'. Watkin's grandiose plan to out-Eiffel Eiffel was laughed at abroad. The American German-language newspaper *Der deutsche Correspondent* wrote: 'The English have forgotten about their fogs. What would be the point of a 2000 foot tower if you could only see its feet?'

In the end the winning design easily met Watkin's sole condition. At almost 1,200ft, 150ft higher than the tower in Paris, it would comfortably break the world record. It actually looked very much like the Eiffel Tower, although it was made of steel, not iron, had six legs and four, not three, platforms. It was to contain a ninety bedroom hotel at first-floor level, restaurants, shops, promenades, Turkish baths, a theatre, a meteorological office, a sanatorium to profit from the pure air high up, a science lab and, right on the top, an observatory, 'because freedom from mists at that altitude would mean the stars could be clearly photographed'.

Watkin chose as his engineer for the project Sir Benjamin Baker, who had been responsible for the Forth Bridge and for transporting Cleopatra's Needle from Egypt to the Thames Embankment. Work began in 1891 and illustrations in newspapers showed just how massive and exciting the project was. Or would be.

'In another eighteen months,' *Freeman's Journal* wrote in 1892, 'London will rejoice in a New Tower of Babel, piercing the skies some 150 feet higher than the renowned Eiffel Tower of Paris. Not only will the Watkin Tower look down 150 feet on the Eiffel Tower, but it will be capable of taking up three times as many passengers at a time.'

The tower was a colossal enterprise that would dominate the North London skyline.

By May 1896 the lifts to the platform were working and the views, stretching as far as Windsor Castle, Epsom Racecourse and the Crystal Palace, were spectacular. But there were no shops or Turkish baths and the lack of amenities reduced the tower's attractiveness. Fewer than 20 per cent of the customers who came to the park in the 1896 season paid to go 155ft up the tower to the first platform, which sadly was as far as the Great Tower in London reached. The company financing it went bankrupt. Watkin was by now suffering from ill health and had virtually retired from public life. Worse was to follow. Incredibly, nobody – not the designers, the directors of the railway, the prestigious engineer or the builders – had carried out a proper survey of the ground underneath the tower. Watkin had simply told the entrants to the competition to assume that the foundations would be sound. The original plan for the tower to have six legs had been altered to four – probably to save money – and the re-distribution of weight together with the London clay proved too much even for the incomplete structure. The Great Tower in London became the Leaning Tower of Pisa, Mark Two. Soon the electric lifts were found to be dangerous and were put out of use. Only a few hardy souls made the climb via stairs which were open to the elements and in its last few months the weekly revenue from the tower ranged from £14 16s. 3d. to 10d. Finally, in 1902, it was declared unsafe and closed to the public. One writer described it as 'peering sadly over a cluster of trees that surrounded it'. For several years it remained on the London skyline, a rusting hulk, still its own constant advertisement, but not as Watkin had intended. It attracted a variety of titles, including the 'Shareholders' Dismay' and the 'London Stump', but one stuck and hung round Sir Edward's neck, 'Watkin's Folly', the name that it is best remembered by even today, when one online article calls Watkin 'The Wally with the Folly'. At the end of 1907 – six years after Watkin's death – the whole structure was dismantled, something that was welcomed in an article in the *Sphere* magazine: 'The general public is grateful because a hideous eyesore is to be removed from a pretty part of the country'. At the end of the process, the legs were dynamited and everything was sold to an Italian scrap-metal firm for £1,200. One photograph shows the remains of the gigantic tower lying on its side with its four legs jutting incongruously up into the air. It has all the dignity of a shot elephant.It was a sad end to a colossal enterprise. Just what a breathtaking scheme the Tower in London was is revealed by a comparison of the heights of the three structures that have occupied the Wembley site over the last 120 years. The twin towers of the first Wembley Stadium were 120ft (38m) high. The arch that soars up over the current stadium is 432ft (133m) high. Watkin's tower reached a maximum height of 154ft (47m) – even at that height it was still London's highest structure – but if he had succeeded it would have reached 1,125ft (358m), almost three times the height of the present arch. A mock-up photograph showing the Tower next to the current stadium makes the point.

Watkin has never been given credit for the vision behind his Wembley project. A daring tourist attraction, miles away from where people lived and worked, was a bold and imaginative concept and was by no means a total failure. Even at the start of the First World War over a hundred sports clubs were still using the facilities of Wembley Park and the golf course had proved so successful that it had been extended to eighteen holes. But the real success of his project only became evident twenty-two years after his death, when his preservation of a great open space in a by now otherwise built-up Wembley made a dramatic new tourist development possible. In 1920, the now derelict Wembley Park was chosen as the site of the British Empire Exhibition, even bigger than the one in Paris a quarter of a century earlier. (Watkin would have been pleased with that.) Its centrepiece was a magnificent sports stadium, ironically with not one but two towers and built on exactly the spot Watkin chose for his tower.

Watkin had not only preserved an enormous open space but a station and this provided easy access from the centre of London for millions of customers to the Exhibition. The original plans for both the Wembley Stadium and the Eiffel Tower had been to demolish them when the exhibitions in Paris and London had closed. Instead Wembley – like the Eiffel Tower – became an icon, just as Watkin had intended with his tower.

Only a few traces of Watkin's great scheme have survived. Wembley Park Station is still on the same site as his two platforms of 1894, but it is now able to cope with 37,500 passengers per hour on major event days. Its name is a visible reminder that Watkin's great plan was not just for an Eiffel Tower in London, though the thousands of London commuters who use the station daily and the excited crowds who get off there on their way to top sporting fixtures are hardly likely to wonder what has happened to the park that gave it its name. When the old stadium was demolished to make way for the current stadium in 2003 the new pitch was dug out at a lower level than its predecessor. A few feet down the builders hit the concrete bases of the legs of Watkin's tower, revealed for the first time in nearly a century. They are still there, under one end of the present pitch.

But the best was yet to come, an idea big enough for Watkin at his most ambitious. In May 2016 Brent Council approved the latest phase in an 85-acre proposal by a major property investment and development company, Quintain. It would have excited Edward Watkin, including the creation of 8 acres of park and gardens. It will turn Wembley Park into one of Europe's biggest regeneration projects, with proposals for

8.8 million sq ft of mixed-use development. Getting a mention on the website of the company responsible for the new Wembley would have particularly pleased him. It acknowledges that it was Watkin the visionary who first saw the potential in a little rural parish called Wembley all those years ago.

Chapter 10

The Railway King

The failures of Watkin's Tower and his Channel tunnel were by any standards spectacular. They inflicted lasting damage on his reputation, even though neither, viewed from the distance of another century, was the complete fiasco which was the verdict in his lifetime. The fate of the tunnel in particular reflects badly not on Watkin but on the blinkered politicians of the time, who stopped him building an icon of British enterprise which would have transformed the history not just of Britain but of Western Europe.

The publicity given to Watkin's failures has overshadowed his other considerable achievements, which included his mastery of Britain's railways during the second half of the nineteenth century. As that magazine article in 1879 showed, he was the 'acknowledged chief' of the country's (and therefore the world's) dominant industry. One of his many nicknames in his lifetime was 'The Railway Doctor' because he was so often sent for to cure sick lines. Another went even further and called him the 'Abernethy of the Railways', after a famous surgeon of the day who was said to be able to cure anything. Not all of his nicknames were as approving as 'Nimble Ned'. Apart from the 'Napoleon' and the 'Machiavelli of the Railways' his enemies called him 'Wrecker Watkin' if a particular scheme was slow to succeed. But whatever names he attracted only underlined his prominence in the railway scene from the 1850s onward, and not only in Britain.

When railways were invented in the early years of the nineteenth century their effect on the civilised world was seismic. No country made the transition from a rural to an industrial economy without building a railway and the railways removed a shackle that had applied to every civilisation in the history of the world. Since the dawn of time, Man had never travelled faster overland than by horse till the railways came. In 1750 the 400-mile coach journey from London to Edinburgh took sixteen days. Now, less than a century later, the train completed it in 8 hours.

But it wasn't only a question of speed. Because of the size of the engines (still measured in horsepower) trains could carry hundreds of passengers. As a result, travel by rail was incredibly cheap, seen at its most extreme in 'the parliamentary trains'. Beginning in 1844, every company was required by law to run at least one service per day on every route in the UK at a special low rate, originally a penny a mile. But even ordinary 'standard class' tickets meant that train journeys were for all the people, not just for ladies and gentlemen in fine coaches. If travel broadens the mind it was the minds of the poorest in the country which expanded most as they left their villages and towns, often for the first time in their lives. The trains changed the political and social balance of society.

Without the power of the trains, the Industrial Revolution would not have been completed. Previously goods could be moved only in small quantities. Even canal transport – and the canals were the motorways of the eighteenth century – was limited to the speed of horses plodding along towpaths. And the canals froze in the winter and dried up in the summer. Now, heavy machinery could be moved in hours to and from the new centres of industry, such as Manchester, all the year round.

The trains were literally the driving force behind Britain's supreme position in the world during Watkin's lifetime. They released and stimulated the astonishing energy and self-confidence of the Victorians, seen at their most dramatic in the Great Exhibition of 1851. It was housed in a massive specially built glass structure in London, the Crystal Palace. Imagine you are building another St Paul's Cathedral. Make it twice as wide and four times as long. That was the Crystal Palace. Its statistics were amazing: 4,000 tons of iron, 400 tons of glass and 600,000 cubic feet of wood. There was a million square feet of floor space and almost a mile of exhibition galleries, which contained 19,000 exhibits. Just as amazing as the finished structure was the speed of its construction. Building did not start till November 1850. Twenty-four weeks later it was ready and opened on time, 1 May 1851, with all its exhibits in place. In its first six months the Great Exhibition attracted 6.2 million visitors, a third of the entire population of Britain. Most of them came by train.

When High Speed 1 reached the Channel Tunnel at the start of the twenty-first century its 67 miles of track had taken ten years to construct. In ten years starting in 1840, the Victorians laid down 4,600 miles of railway. When the Great Western Railway decided to change the width of its tracks it had to install a new rail on all their existing routes. The last stretch was from London to Penzance via Bristol, Exeter and Plymouth, 177 miles in all. It was started and finished in a single weekend.

Victorian Britain dazzled the world with its inventions and its new machines, including the inspirational new railways. Even men of distinction caught the railway bug. The Earl of Derby made a speech in which he said: 'We look forward today to a complete railway line from Paris to Peking.' The occasion was opening of the St Helens to Wigan Junction Railway. A headline in one newspaper in August 1846 captures the thrill of the Railway Age: 'GREAT MONSTER TRAINS TO THE NORTH OF ENGLAND'. The article goes on:

> The vicinity of the Euston terminus of the North-Western Railway was on Friday evening the scene of much excitement by the departure of two very great monster trains for Newcastle, York, Darlington, and other Northern towns. They were the returning excursion trains that arrived in London late last Monday evening and the number of persons who availed themselves of this trip may be judged from the following rate of fares: From Newcastle, there and back, first class, £2.2s; second class £1.10s; third class, £1.1s, the entire distance being more than 600 miles. The first train left shortly after seven o'clock. It comprised nearly fifty carriages and conveyed more than 2000 passengers. Newcastle was expected to be reached in about fifteen hours.

The second half of the century was the boom era for the railways. During the period when Watkin was at the height of his power, the statistics become staggering. In 1881 the railways employed 206,301 men and 706 women. They owned 12,790 locomotives and 28,190 passenger carriages. In England, Scotland and Wales there were 367,492 goods wagons in use on 15,563 miles of track. Total passenger numbers were 586 million. One other, less dry statistic shows the size of the railway industry. At the main entrance to Victoria Station in Manchester is a memorial plaque commemorating the employees of one of the smaller railway companies, the Lancashire and Yorkshire, who were killed in the First World War. It contains nearly 1,500 names.

What guaranteed Watkin's special place in the newspapers was his genius for rescuing lines threatened with bankruptcy, his flair for publicity and his obvious relish for confrontations with his rivals in the other railway companies. But behind the flashy headlines it was the extraordinary number of railway companies that he ruled that gave him the power to command Britain's railway system. His influence stretched from Liverpool, Manchester and Sheffield to Swansea and London and the South Coast. He was chairman of eight railway companies in Britain and director of a further thirteen. To these twenty-one must be added his shareholding in many others. In these he was never passive, as the minutes of annual shareholders' meetings show. It is an astonishing picture, bearing in mind that he was always involved at a senior level, active in an industry that was growing explosively, never just ticking over. What lifts his record from the amazing to the incredible, however, is that at the same time he found the energy to be involved in the development of railways abroad, in four continents. After rescuing the Grand Trunk Railway of Canada from bankruptcy and building it up into the longest railway in the world, he almost incidentally advised on the railway systems of Honduras in the Caribbean, Athens in Europe, the Belgian Congo in Africa, and India.

Watkin was not just interested in collecting trophies, though the sheer number of companies he was involved in suggests he was not averse to this. He was always conscious of the bigger picture. The man who returned from Canada after rescuing the Grand Trunk was not the same man who had gone there on sick leave in 1861. He had found in Canada a country 'large enough to breed large ideas' and while he was there he had grown used to painting on a big canvas and meeting major politicians. The epitaph on his gravestone is from the Bible: 'Seest thou a man diligent in his business? He shall stand before kings.'

His aim in Britain was what a perceptive obituary in *The Times* called 'the building up of a great railway system which should overshadow the largest and most important of our existing systems'. As with the Grand Trunk in Canada, Watkin never pretended that his only interest was in knocking existing railways into shape. His master plan was to link three major railways: the MSLR, the Metropolitan and the SER. In a document he had written back in 1860 he had referred to 'the importance of obtaining independent access to London' for the MSLR. (He was only its general secretary at the time.) In evidence to Parliament a few months after he became chairman of 'The Met' he spoke of his determination: 'to connect the new Sheffield line with the Metropolitan' and in his first public reference to an even grander scheme he went on: 'and further extend it through London to a junction with the South Eastern'. Not surprisingly, he did not emphasise at this early stage that his real aim was to drive on from the South Coast of England through a new Channel tunnel and head for Paris, Baghdad and ultimately India.

When Watkin became chairman of the MSLR in 1864 it was a tiddler compared with the big fish down south and the giant he was creating in British North America. Juicy profits were to be made from the lines into London and that is what the MSLR lacked. The three established major companies, the London North Western, the Great Northern and the Great Eastern, had carved up the traffic to the capital between them and had a cosy shared monopoly – or so they thought. For its own London traffic, both passenger and freight, the MSLR had been allowed to use lines owned by the Big Three – but at a price. Even as late as 1891 it was still paying two-thirds of its London revenues to them for the privilege of using their tracks. It also lacked the prestige of a terminus of its own in the capital city of the greatest country in the world. But like a brilliant footballer, Watkin had spotted a gap in his opponents' defence and in 1891 he attacked. His bill to extend the MSLR south was tabled. It was the birth of what was to become the Great Central Railway, running right through the middle of England and heading for London. The battle to gain access to London was hard and often vicious. (The painstaking detail is set out in the two Watkin biographies.) His grand plans could easily (and accurately) be described as jam tomorrow, at the expense of this year's dividends – and often next year's as well. The other three railway companies fought him not just through Parliament but through the courts and at shareholders' meetings with arguments designed to appeal to the desire for jam today. Only his authority, his parliamentary experience, his wiliness and his skill and courage at handling angry meetings carried the day. Yet it would be a mistake to think that his eventual victory was inevitable. In the middle of the battle, when everything was going wrong, when friends were deserting him and enemies were dancing prematurely on his grave Watkin showed his character in his stubborn refusal to admit defeat. His enemies mocked him with names for the MSLR ('Money, Sunk and Lost') and eventually the Great Central ('Gone Completely'). But victory was finally his. It had taken him over thirty years since first joining the board of the MSLR for him to become a major London player. But the battle broke his health.

First in his sights was the SER, one of Britain's earliest railways and covering the whole of Kent, East Sussex and the London suburbs. In 1866 its finances were in dire straits and it was being torn apart by disputes. Watkin was asked to take over as chairman to bring an end to these. It was an appointment full of irony since his subsequent thirty year reign was marked by constant disputes between the SER and the rival London, Chatham and Dover Railway or rather between the two chairmen, Watkin and James Staats Forbes. They were two of a kind, big beasts of the jungle, who ruled like monarchs. (It was widely believed that it was Forbes who worked on Sir Garnet Wolseley to oppose Watkin's Channel tunnel.)

The SER was an established railway, with a route leading directly from London to the English Channel. This fitted neatly into Watkin's master plan and once he had gained control of the SER he turned his sights to where the innovation had to be, further north. What he had realised was that although the Big Three railway companies had covered the routes into London from the northwest, the north and the east, they had left a gap through the centre. He decided to fill the gap with a railway that would both link with the SER and push north to meet the MSLR moving south. The London Metropolitan Railway ticked both boxes – and its chaotic finances were crying out for some medicine from the Railway Doctor.

The Met had opened in 1863 to serve the inner London suburbs and link the main-line railway termini of Paddington, Euston and King's Cross to the City. A plaque near Madame Tussaud's in Marylebone Road in London records that it was the world's first underground railway, intended to relieve the traffic on the streets of central London by creating, in Watkin's words, 'underground omnibuses'. In 1872 Watkin was asked to nurse the Met back to health by becoming its chairman. He set about his task with his usual gusto. The directors were forced to retire and a new auditor – one of the best of the time – was appointed. The new broom can be seen in one of Watkin's memos in 1874: 'The work seems only to dawdle on. I see nothing that looks like "push". We want energy and work, not reports and talk.'

As with the Grand Trunk in Canada, however, improving the efficiency of the Met was only the start of Watkin's vision. The key development under Watkin's chairmanship was that he changed the Met from being just an underground railway in London. He was single-minded in his aim to extend it further and further to the north – and overland – as part of his plan for a single railway from Manchester to the South Coast. He was gradually changing it, in John Greaves' words, into 'a main line railway with an underground system as a southern appendage'. Even when its development out of London was complete, however, there was still a gap of 83 miles between its most northerly station at Quainton Road in Buckinghamshire and the most southerly station of the MSLR, at Annesley Junction, 6 miles north of Nottingham. Closing that gap with what came to be known as the London Extension was the most difficult phase of Watkin's pioneering work but when it was complete he had achieved his strategic aim. He had created a railway from Manchester to London, the Great Central, the last main line into the capital for over a century until High Speed 1 was built for Eurostar. Its completion was a testament not only to Watkin's strategic vision but also to his tactical skills and political nous. Often undervalued and the only main line to have been closed by the Beeching Axe in the 1960s, it reached the height of its importance in conveying men and materials during the First World War. The prime minister at the time, Lloyd George, said that without the Great Central Britain would not have won that war.

The first sod of the London Extension was cut in the garden of a private house in Alpha Road, St John's Wood, on 14 November 1894 but the lead-in to that day had called for all the qualities of persistence, cajolery and wiliness that Watkin had honed for the previous fifty years of his public life, starting with the campaign for public parks in Manchester. He lobbied people he knew in business and politics and socially, such as a former Solicitor General (who was also his uncle), a former Home Secretary and Baron Rothschild, whose banking family had been customers of Absalom Watkin in Manchester all those years previously. With his finger on the pulse of local government decision-making he worked on the councils of Nottingham, Leicester and Rugby, all cities which would profit from a through line to London with their own major new stations. By early 1891 his plans were in place, the land was earmarked and the new line was ready to be put before Parliament.

Then came an obstacle that it seemed at first must defeat him. Tantalisingly, it involved a small piece of land only a few hundred yards short of his final destination, which was to be a new London terminus at Marylebone. But this was not just any old land. It was in St John's Wood, one of the capital's most select corners, home to a large number of very rich people, a community of highly regarded artists and, most daunting of all, cricket's awesome Holy of Holies, Lord's. Early in 1890 the unbelievable news broke that Watkin was going to put a bill before Parliament which would ruin the neighbourhood. It would provide for a railway line right through St John's Wood, carrying not only passengers but 'coal, manure, fish and other abominations' in a cutting open to the air. Even worse, the line would destroy the sacred turf of Lord's cricket ground.

For centuries cricket had been England's major team sport. The Football Association, formed to draw up standard rules for what was seen as a largely working man's game, was only twenty-seven years old and the Football League, set up to establish a regular competition, had been in existence only two years. On the other hand, the Marylebone Cricket Club (MCC), with its home at Lord's, had been established in 1787 and was the governing body of cricket throughout the civilised world, defined for many as anywhere cricket was played. Watkin himself once referred to the Secretary of the MCC in a speech: 'There are five estates of the realm now: Queen, one; House of Lords, two; House of Commons, three; the Press, four; and Lord's cricket ground and Mr Perks, five.'

Lord's was a bastion of privilege. Watkin was about to take on the most influential group of people in England, including members of the royal family, aristocrats in the House of Lords, bankers and landowners and the members of the MCC. To say that there was horror at his proposals would be to understate the sense of outrage felt by the MCC members and local residents, including the artists. One MP told Parliament:

> Does anyone imagine if the hon. Baronet (Sir E. Watkin) gets a foothold in Lord's, he will not eventually take the whole ground? If this railway is not a sham, if it is to have any traffic at all, the terminus must be a larger one than that which is now proposed, and to effect this Lord's must be acquired altogether. But what is to happen to cricket players even supposing the terminus remains as proposed? Fancy a match between Oxford and Cambridge, or Eton and Harrow, with the galaxy of beauty which is always to be found at Lord's on such occasions. If there is a south wind, dust and dirt will be blown from this terminus, and not only be a great inconvenience, but will damage the beautiful and costly dresses of the ladies.

At first the MCC were so confident that Watkin could not win that the club was content just to support the local community of St John's Wood in its fight to stop the railway. A headline in the local paper read 'Birth of an Abomination' and the Marylebone and St John's Wood United Committee of Opposition was quickly formed to thwart Watkin's plans. The MCC donated £50 'towards preliminary opposition by inhabitants of the district'. Soon however, as the archives at Lord's show in their records of correspondence and in the minute book setting out the club committee's decisions, it became clear that Sir Edward Watkin meant business. He would have to be opposed by all the means at the disposal of the Club. Noble loins were girded, a special sub-committee was formed (it met at St James's Palace) and a parliamentary agent was appointed, the MCC Auditor, who had considerable experience in parliamentary procedure. Plans were made for a petition. One of the Archive letters said: 'The petition will cover sheets of parchment. What think you? Get it headed by HRH PW [i.e. the Prince of Wales, the future King Edward VII] and have the Duke of Baccleuch or such like at the top.' Another suggestion was that 'a little advertisement in *The Times*, *Morning Post* and sporting papers would bring people to sign in flocks'. The Trustees of the Club (led by the Earl of Sefton and the Earl of Bessborough) prepared a statement to present to Parliament when Watkin's railway bill was discussed. This included a paragraph which described the MCC in almost mystical terms:

> The Marylebone Cricket Club is practically the Parliament of Cricket whose laws, though not necessarily binding on, are, as a matter of fact, followed by Cricket Clubs almost universally, and it has been well said that 'Countries which were not known to exist when wickets were pitched at Guildford in the reign of Henry Vlll, take their law from Lord's Cricket Ground and regard Marylebone as the Omphalos [a stone in the Temple of Apollo at Delphi in Ancient Greece that was believed to mark the centre point of the earth] of Cricket.'

The Committee also decided to employ a Mr Galbraith, who was said to be the best engineer of the day. He would demonstrate that the proposed railway would be a technical disaster. He would be a 'capital witness', not only because of his professional qualifications but because he was 'a member of Lords, a man bitterly opposed to the Bill, having regard to his own property in St John's Wood'. Just how important it was to defeat the bill is shown in a line in one letter from the MCC Auditor: 'Probably 20 lines from London to the North are better for you and me than [Watkin's] 3 or 4 but Lord's is sacred.'

One magazine article proposed that Briggs, the Lancashire bowler, should be sent to 'cripple the ruthless baronet'. The most famous cricketer in history, W.G. Grace, said that 'the thought of a railway line running through the chief bulwark of our national pastime was repellent'. A cartoon in *Punch* showed the massed ranks of MCC members, armed with cricket stumps, resisting the advance of a steam train and an army of navvies across the ground. They are led on a horse by Grace, like a knight of old.

In the face of all this anger, Watkin showed just how skilled a negotiator he could be. He defeated the opposition by advancing on three fronts. First of all, he showed a subtlety that surprised people who saw him only as a bully. He emphasised how much cricket meant to him. Was not a member of his family A.N. Hornby, formerly captain of England and Lancashire, second only to Grace in reputation? Hornby is now immortalised in a nostalgic poem by Francis Thompson looking back to happier days at Lord's:

> For the field is full of shades as I near a shadowy coast,
> And a ghostly batsman plays to the bowling of a ghost,
> And I look through my tears on a soundless-clapping host
> As the run stealers flicker to and fro
> To and fro:
> O my Hornby and my Barlow long ago!

Hornby was actually the son-in-law of Watkin's second wife but that was near enough to be useful and he did attend Watkin's funeral in 1901. Anyway, said Watkin, there was no suggestion that the sacred turf would be dug up. The only land affected would be one corner of the practice ground. (It had formerly been Henderson's Nurseries, known also as Pineapples because that was where the best pineapples in Britain were grown. It is still called The Nursery today and is where promising young cricketers are nurtured.) Disturbance to that one corner would be only temporary, while a tunnel, not an open cutting, was dug then covered over. The contract would stipulate that all work would be completed 'between the month of September in one year and April in the following year', in other words, during cricket's close season.

But Watkin's master stroke involved some land right next to Lord's. It was occupied by the Clergy Orphan School for Girls. He would buy the land, re-house the orphanage and knock down the buildings. Would the MCC then kindly accept the land as a donation? He would remove all the rubble and lay turf 'to the satisfaction of the MCC Engineer'. The MCC committee recognised a bargain when they saw one. Anyway, they had privately received advice that they might not be able to defeat Watkin's parliamentary bill since they could not stop the march of his railway into London. The mood of the minutes began to change. They recorded that Watkin was prepared to 'deal most liberally' with the Club. The MCC authorised their agent to carry on negotiations and to ask the railway company to put up an unofficial proposal. Within just five weeks the outrage which had been first recorded in the minutes of 12 January 1891 had begun to evaporate. At a meeting of the committee held on 19 February terms were agreed with the railway company, subject to the approval of a special meeting of the membership, to be held on 6 April. That, however, proved to be by no means a formality. A minute early in March recorded that 'many verbal and written remonstrances against any bargain with Watkin and the Manchester, Sheffield and Lincolnshire Railway' had been received. Over 180 members turned up for the special meeting, 2½ times the number that had attended the previous AGM. There were complaints that the meeting should have been called much earlier in the process. One member said that the committee had been 'Watkinised'. An amendment opposing the Committee's proposal for agreement with the railway company was moved but was defeated by 150 votes to 24. The Committee's relief is evident in the recording of the subsequent approval of an agreement. The Secretary, whose style is usually dry and formal, writes that the majority in favour was 'enormous'.

Matters did not end there, however. At a second general meeting held on 7 December a resolution to oppose the agreement was defeated by a narrower majority, 96 to 65. However, one of the most respected members, Sir Henry James, later Lord James of Hereford, the Solicitor General in one of Gladstone's Cabinets, said that the club would look foolish if it tried to go back on its original decision.

That was the end of the MCC's fight, though there were other opponents. The artists of St John's Wood tried to continue their campaign but they were now on their own and out of their depth in a fight with the big boys, or rather the big boy from 'oop' north. Their case was not helped by one of them who said in an interview that the vibration of the trains would stop her being able to paint straight. A local minister warned in a sermon that digging up the ground would enrage the Devil.

But the fight to get his London Extension through Parliament had exhausted Watkin, who was now 75 years old. By May 1894 he was so ill with heart trouble that he had to resign the chairmanships of the three railway companies that had been his life.

By the following November (it must have been painful for him to have fallen six months short), however, Watkin's railway bill had passed all its parliamentary stages and that first sod of the London Extension was cut by the wife of Watkin's successor as chairman of the MSLR, the Earl of Wharncliffe. The report in the *Manchester Guardian* is full of that delight in detail and artefacts typical of the age:

> A substantial structure had been erected over the spot, and the inside was decorated with red baize and trophies of flags. Sir Edward Watkin presented to Lady Wharncliffe the spade and barrow to be used in turning and removing the first turf. The barrow, of English oak, was decorated with silver fittings, and bore at the back a large shield containing an inscription. The feet of the barrow were of solid silver engraved with acanthus leaves blended with honeysuckle. Her ladyship entered within the roped enclosure and released with the spade the already loosened turf. Amid loud cheers the Countess dropped the square of turf into the barrow, which she wheeled in front of the dais. The Earl, coming forward on the platform, thanked the company in the name of his wife, for their attendance. Sir E Watkin MP, who next rose, was welcomed with an enthusiasm that evidently affected him deeply. The whole company present rose and cheered him for some time.

Watkin was well enough to say only a few words. One newspaper report said that the occasion 'will, in all probability, prove to be his last appearance in public life' and continued: 'To those familiar with Sir Edward's vivid personality, his rapid step, his mobile countenance and his peremptory speech, it was sad to see on this crowning occasion the old man seated silent on his chair at the banquet, or tottering feebly to and from his place, looking with unresponsive regard upon the faces of old familiar friends.'

Five years later, on 9 March 1899, Marylebone Station opened for business, a year after the tunnel under Lord's was completed and just in time for the start of the new cricket season. An advertisement shortly after the opening emphasised how up-to-date it was: 'Extensive stables built on the most modern principles. The electric light is used throughout and accommodation is provided for 700 horses.'

Perhaps because of a neighbourhood that includes some of the wealthiest residences in London and the headquarters of the MCC, Marylebone Station has always been seen as different from the other main-line stations in the capital. It still has a genteel air about it. The poet John Betjeman compared it to 'a public library from Nottingham which has unexpectedly found itself in London'. A writer in 1933 described a visitor seeing Marylebone as:

> … the quietest and most dignified of stations, where the porters go on tiptoe, where the barrows are rubber-tyred and the trains sidle mysteriously in and out with only the faintest of toots upon their whistles so as not to disturb the signalman. There he bought a ticket to Aylesbury from a man who whispered that the cost was nine-and-six, and that the train would probably start from Number 5 platform.

Behind the gentle facade however, the construction of the new station and its hotel and goods yards meant that over 6,000 local people lost their homes and many, in spite of the law that was supposed to protect them, were never compensated. One of the houses that was demolished had belonged to the famous female novelist Amantine-Lucile-Aurore Dupin, who wrote under the pen name George Sand. A reporter interviewed the local postman, who said he remembered George and his very fine singing voice. One substantial house, ready for demolition but still untouched, had an enormous building erected in its back garden with 'Manchester, Sheffield and Lincolnshire Railway London Extension 1894' on its front arch. It highlighted the change coming in a quiet residential neighbourhood. The road opposite the new railway building led to Omega Place.

Another house that was demolished had been nearby in Alpha Road. It had belonged to Jerome K. Jerome, who later became famous as the author of *Three Men in a Boat*. Thirty years later he remembered: 'It was in a quiet by-road through which no traffic passed; it was surrounded by big houses standing in their own grounds; it was quite detached, with a garden all round it.' When the railway company offered him a total of £750 for compulsory purchase, Jerome, who had just spent £800 on renovations, took them to court. Among the witnesses that supported him was W.S. Gilbert, half of the famous musical pair. Unfortunately, the judge, according to Jerome, was biased against him. 'Whenever Mr Littler, QC, winked – and he winked frequently – the jury leaned over, nodded back at him, and tittered. When he made a joke they roared; when he sneered they tossed their heads contemptuously.' Jerome may have had a point: the court awarded him only £500 for the house and made him pay costs.

The building of the new station just off the Marylebone Road brought about a personal tragedy. Half a mile away in Aberdeen Place is a beautiful and ornate Edwardian restaurant, conspicuously out of place in a residential area. It was originally called 'The Crown' but in 1987 it was renamed 'Crocker's Folly', in honour of the man who built it. Frank Crocker spent a fortune on designing The Crown as a luxury hotel to serve the Great Central's London terminus – which he believed would be built in nearby St John's Wood Road, next to the cricket ground. It wasn't. His gamble failed, he was ruined and he died prematurely – though not as some reports have it in his marooned folly. The sceptical architect who designed the hotel placed a bust of a Roman emperor in the bar. Caracalla was famous for architectural excesses and insanity. Crocker's ghost is said to haunt the site.

In March 1899 a grand ceremony marked not only the opening of the new station at Marylebone and the completion of the line but also the official transformation of the MSLR into the Great Central Railway. Lunch was served to over 800 guests. The chairman said that the London Extension was 'the greatest railway enterprise authorised by Parliament for more than fifty years'. He continued that the Company had spent £12 million on the Extension – the shareholders must have seen that as a lot of jam but tomorrow had finally arrived. He paid tribute to:

> ... the energy and genius of one man, and that man is Sir Edward
> Watkin. (Loud cheers.) I congratulate him upon the fact that he has
> been able to see the completion of an undertaking of which he is

the father and the grandfather. (Applause.) … It is a line which has gone through much tribulation. We are all pleased that Sir Edward has been able to join us to see the crown placed on a work which has occupied so much of his busy life (Cheers).

In fact, Watkin was by now so ill that he was able to attend only in a wheelchair. At the end of the ceremony he said to a friend: 'My work is now done but I am thankful that I have lived to see this day.'

A new plaque in the concourse of Marylebone Station, now managed by Chiltern Railways, marks its place in railway history as the terminus of the last main line into London for over a century and commemorates the man who created it. The road leading to the station, Great Central Street, and the station's address, Great Central House, recall its origins.

Next to the station is the Landmark Hotel. The owners are proud of the building's heritage, including its connection with the Great Central Railway and Watkin. At the top of the grand staircase in the reception hall is the original magnificent stained glass window containing the insignia of the railway and its motto 'Forward'. Over the stairs leading down to the Great Central Bar is a board setting out the history of the building. The first entry records that the hotel was created by Sir Edward Watkin as the 'last great Victorian railway hotel'. In the Landmark's archives is a sumptuous leather-bound book published in March 1899 to commemorate the opening of the station. One of its specially drawn pictures shows the scene as the first train is leaving. Sir Edward Watkin can be glimpsed standing in the crowd. Actually, because he was in failing health after his heart attacks, he would not have been well enough to leave his wheelchair. Closer examination reveals that the image is copied from an earlier photo of Watkin. It is a personal tribute by an unknown artist to the creator of the new railway.

The Great Central Railway was the jewel in the crown of Watkin's railway career in Britain. It was a testament to his vision and his determination not to be beaten. It had been built to, for Britain, an exceptionally high engineering standard, ready for its trains to carry freight on the Continent's tracks. It had no bends, only slight curves and its maximum gradient was 1:176. It was ready for the double-decker trains of Switzerland and Germany, still unknown in Britain. By the time of its opening, however, Watkin's ill health had forced him to resign from the committees of all his railway companies except the Great Central, which had incorporated the MSLR, the dynamic new company he had joined forty-six years previously. It must have retained echoes for him as his special baby. He remained on the board of the Great Central till December 1900. Sixteen weeks later, he was dead.

Before we leave the railway section of the Edward Watkin story, however, there is a remarkable footnote to be added, one that has been ignored till now. It occurred under his chairmanship of the Metropolitan, the last in that trio of railway companies that were the links in his vision of constructing a railway from Manchester to Paris and beyond. Two of his actions on behalf of the Met contributed to perhaps the most significant residential development in London in the twentieth century. He has never been given full credit for the part he played in a housing boom there which put a new word into the English language: Metroland.

Exploiting the gap in central England to create a new main line into London was an amazingly confident move. But bringing an underground railway to the surface north of the capital was a stroke of genius. It was not only central to Watkin's master plan for a railway to Paris. It opened up enormous untapped areas of housing land to what we would now call commuters by putting them within easy reach of the Met's new stations and central London. Watkin created his own customers. For the next thirty years thousands of desirable houses were built in pretty tree-lined suburbs such as Harrow, Pinner, Rickmansworth and Chorley Wood, each with nice shops and nice parks. It was dubbed 'Metroland' and the name caught on. One poem ran:

> I know a land where the wild flowers grow
> Near, near at hand if by train you go,
> Metroland, Metroland.

A popular song of 1920 had the title 'My Little Metro-land Home' and another extolled the virtues of the Poplar estate at Ruislip with the twee if clunky assertion that, 'It's a very short distance by rail on the Met/And at the gate you'll find waiting sweet Violet'. In Evelyn Waugh's novel *Decline and Fall*, published in 1928, the Hon. Margot Beste-Chetwynd takes Viscount Metroland as her second husband and she appears as Lady Metroland in his *Vile Bodies* two years later. The French borrowed the word for the underground system in Paris, le Métropolitain, always shortened to le Métro.

Metroland was marketed as a paradise, ideal for a day trip away from the smoke and noise of London or better still a wonderful place to live in. It caught the mood of families that were enjoying new wealth and became captivated by the ease and speed of transport into the countryside on the Metro's trains, as two of its advertisements show:

> The estate has the particular advantage of being self-contained and wherever you choose a house on this estate you may rest assured that you will be surrounded by other ES Reid houses. You may be sure that you will not have a nasty cheap mass-production house anywhere near you to lower the value of your property.
>
> The ladies pull down the blinds in the First Class and flick over the pages of Vogue or The Lady. Retired businessmen contemplate a day on the golf course at Moor Park or a trip to town to visit their clubs and old acquaintances whilst they look at the latest events from Germany in The Morning Post. But nobody really cares. It's summer and the wayside banks are full of flowers.

This advertisement appeared a few days before war was declared in the summer of 1914: 'The Kaiser's up to something but in the meantime, before we enjoy the new war that's just around the corner, let's go out on Bank Holiday Monday to the Chilterns.'

Watkin's extension of the Metropolitan Underground was followed by another stroke of genius but one that has never received the attention it deserves. It was his bequest to the directors of the railway in the form of a legal 'sleeper' which boosted the company's profits many years after his death. It was another example of his considerable parliamentary skills and his ability on occasions (as with his behind-the-scenes work in Canada) to act effectively away from the glare of publicity which usually accompanied his activities.

While piloting his Metropolitan Railway Extension Bill through Parliament, he quietly inserted an extra section into the new Act. In view of its consequences it is amazing – and a tribute to his wiliness – that none of his opponents realised what he was up to. Since 1845 railway companies had been required by Parliament to dispose of all unused land adjacent to their lines within ten years of the opening of a new service. That law remained in force well into the twentieth century but to its surprise and ultimately great profit the Metropolitan Railway discovered that it did not apply to them, simply because Watkin had included a unique provision in his bill. The company would be allowed to retain all surplus lands, 'whenever required, including those acquired in the future'. All that was needed was for the company to 'reasonably believe' that they might need the land for new railways or for 'other purposes'. These two innocent-sounding words were to have tremendous consequences for they gave the Metropolitan unlimited power to grant building leases and sell ground rents for the surplus lands next to their tracks. They became part of blossoming and highly profitable Metroland.

The special provisions of the 1873 Act were the work of Watkin alone, drawing on his experience as an MP and his mastery of detail to such an extent that he was able to steer the legislation through the intricacies of parliamentary procedure without attracting attention. Bequeathing to the Met large chunks of railway land that enabled the directors to profit from the housing boom in the Chilterns was such a mouth-watering windfall that before the company dared to exploit it during the 1920s they instructed their lawyers to check with Parliament that it was legal. It was, and as a result Metroland should be added to Watkin's list of triumphs which he did not live to see.

The Grand Trunk Railway in Canada, the Central Railway from Manchester to London, including Metroland, Watkin's active involvement in a long list of other railway companies in Britain, his work for railways on the Continent of Europe and in Africa and India are an amazing catalogue of achievements by one man and in their effects they far outweigh his two spectacular failures. At the front of the collection of newspaper obituaries commissioned by Watkin's daughter Harriette, which form part of his archive in the Chetham's Library, Manchester, is a photograph of her father. It carries the caption: 'The Railway King.' Nobody has worn that crown since.

Chapter 11

The Final Years

A re-evaluation of Edward Watkin's place in history is long overdue. Before making it though, we need to complete his own story by recording the sad, slow decline in his personal and public life as he approached old age.

A 4,000-word article about Watkin which appeared in 1891 in *The World*, an American newspaper published in New York, is a skilful and in part sympathetic summary of his life. After an opening paragraph referring to this 'seventy-two year-old gentleman who works, works and has accomplished great things for England' his achievements are set out in full. There is admiration for 'the dynamic powers of his brain' and references to his possessing the 'energy of a demon'. He is 'the most concrete expression of the spirit of his times'. Yet the headline over the article reads: 'A Munchausen of Deeds. Sir Edward William Watkin and his Wonderful Work'. The reference is to a fictional character famous for his exaggerated stories about himself and the general tone of the article is mildly sceptical. At the time it was written Watkin's tower at Wembley was still under construction. It is described with something less than enthusiasm as his 'pet scheme'. The Channel tunnel is a 'most wonderful scheme' but it is a 'submarine hole', and there is a long list of its 'calm and hard-headed' opponents, balanced only by Watkin's 'strong belief' in its likely success and a reference to his 'most reasonable hope' that the tunnel and his other projects will be realised.

The article appeared at the start of what was to be the last decade of Watkin's life, when the great fixer was at last beginning to look vulnerable. The failure of the Great Tower at London, coming soon after the fiasco of the Channel tunnel, hurt Watkin deeply. His public reputation meant everything to him. What must have made the failures harder to bear was that they coincided with a period of private unhappiness, beginning with the loss of his wife, Mary, on 8 March 1888.

Watkin was deeply affected by the death of a woman he described as not only a 'loving and devoted wife' but as his 'best friend and truest counsellor'. In the forty-three years of their marriage she had been the rock on which he had relied during a turbulent career. After the references to Mary in his own diaries, ending in 1848, and in Absalom's diary, no personal descriptions of Lady Watkin in the next forty years have survived.

During that period the only information we have about her is in newspaper reports of her public life, as it was recorded, for example, in the local paper when she and Edward threw open Rose Hill and its gardens to the local residents on special occasions. Such reports, as was the norm in the second half of the nineteenth century, described her as second fiddle to her eminent husband in his public life. In reality though Mary was a very able woman, described by the family solicitor as 'a woman of remarkable business capacity'.

Shortly after her funeral Watkin wrote 'A Memoir' of his wife. It was a private document, intended only for the family and close friends, but a copy of the original is in the Chetham's Library. It bears out the comment that Watkin had made in his diary forty-four years earlier, shortly after he met her: 'She is a good manager'. He says that she was 'essentially a woman of business, grasping the complicated problems' of his daily work and he refers to her 'great constructive and administrative capacity'. He picks out two of her achievements. 'To her was largely owing the creation of Provident Savings Banks of the Manchester, Sheffield and Lincolnshire, South Eastern and Metropolitan Railways through which more than a million of money of the savings of working people has passed.' More personal was that 'she herself planned and saw to the carrying out of a large extension and a complete remodelling' of Rose Hill. Absalom had developed the Watkin home from a run-down little farmhouse into a large house. Under Mary's control it became a villa with an art gallery, a ballroom and a grand dining room, fit for the entertainment and accommodation of prime ministers and other great figures of Victorian society. More personally, she was responsible for the family's finances and their bank account. The failures and successes of Edward's many schemes must have generated quite a number of entries.

In her last years, Watkin wrote, Mary had 'suffered from a disease which slowly but surely undermined her strength'. (Her death certificate records the cause as diabetes mellitus and congestion of the lungs.) She had been unable to appear at the ball that he organised to celebrate her 64th birthday in January 1887. By the end of that year she was only able to go out into the garden in a bath chair. 'The last four or five months of her life were spent in her bedroom, for the most part propped up in her chair, for often she was unable to lie down in bed, owing to difficulty in breathing'. He missed many business meetings in order to be with her. In a letter to Gladstone in December 1887 Watkin said that his wife was somewhat stronger and was hoping to receive her grandchildren on Christmas Day. In the February she organised the distribution of shawls and new half crowns to thirty older women from Northenden village and 'a good plain dinner in the Servants' Hall'. That was, however, her final public act.

In late nineteenth-century Britain, the norm was for people to die at home, surrounded by their family. Watkin was not with his wife when she died and the careful choice of words as he describes her last days suggests that his absence had made him feel guilty:

> Her last hours were very peaceful. On 6 March 1888 her husband, who now, except for a few brief and hurried journeys, rarely left her, was obliged to go to London on urgent business and his place was taken by his daughter.... On the morning of the seventh no apprehensions were felt and a telegram to that effect was sent to her husband. As the day went on she improved greatly. A telegram to this effect was sent to her husband, who, in consequence, changed the plans he had made for coming back, and decided to remain to finish his business the next morning. About five o'clock it became clear that the end could not be far off – it could only be a question of days. It was felt right to send for her husband.

Sadly, Watkin could not get home till 4 o'clock in the morning of the 8th. Mary had died 3 hours earlier.

Mary's funeral, described in the *Stockport Advertiser* in a report of more than 2,000 words, reflects Sir Edward's high reputation at the time. Expressions of sympathy were received from the King of the Belgians, Gladstone, the prime minister, a succession of earls and lords, the mayors or lord mayors of London, Manchester, Folkestone and Hythe, and representatives of the American and French governments. Watkin's grief was evident. 'During the time of the internment a drizzling snow fell, but many watched the final obsequies with uncovered heads, among whom we observed Sir Edward himself, whose pent-up grief found relief in a copious flow of tears as the body was lowered into its lasting resting place.'

Although Edward was a very different character from his father, one thing they had in common was their restless nature. But where Absalom had failed to find stability through his marriage his son had succeeded. Mary's death could well explain the failures in his public life in his last years. He was to a certain extent rudderless without her good judgement, most dramatically in his decision to build his tower without securing enough finance or checking the geological foundations of Wembley Park.

Six of the stained glass windows in St Wilfrid's Church in Northenden were paid for by Edward. One shows three saints named Mary – Mary Magdalen, the Virgin Mary and Mary of Bethany. In one corner is a miniature portrait of Lady Mary Watkin. The implication is clear.

At several points the article in *The World* refers to Watkin's personal sadness. 'In a big house up in Cheshire … he lives alone, with his picture gallery and his big empty rooms'. 'Social life at Rose Hill is naturally not what it was when Lady Watkin was at her husband's side.' 'When she died … a deep shadow fell upon Rose Hill, Northenden, which has never lifted. Such a loss cannot be repaired, and none but the ceaselessly active mind of Sir Edward Watkin can know how much was taken from his life when her place at his side was left vacant.'

Watkin's last years were lonely. In addition to the loss of his wife, his parents, his sister and his three brothers were all dead. His two children, Alfred and Harriette, were both still alive but had left home when they married. Edward was always publicly loyal to his son, Alfred, and made him the sole executor of his estate. But Alfred must have been a disappointment to his father, who set great store by achievement and public acclaim. Apart from a short and disastrous parliamentary career, which he owed entirely to his father's desire to keep control of the town of Grimsby, Alfred seems to have done little with his life. He took on various minor jobs, each with railway companies controlled by his father, and became a qualified engine driver in 1865. One of the few photographs of him that have survived shows him in the cab of an engine and wearing a driver's cap. In June 1873 he was allowed to drive his father's train as it carried the Shah of Persia on a visit to London.

After his father's death Sir Alfred lost no time in selling off the family home to a businessman who also had no interest in Northenden or Rose Hill. Absalom and Edward's magnificent library was broken up and sold at auction and Alfred went back to his home in Folkestone, Lanchester House. Its name reflects his obsession with Lanchester cars. One shows him seated at the wheel of a Lanchester car in front of his prominently named Lanchester House. In his will he mentioned specially his 'motor cars which shall be in or about my said residence at the time of my death'. He made special provision for 'the gold enamelled and diamond brooch designed by me being a model of a Lanchester Motor Car'.

Watkin had made sure that both his children had what was called in those days 'a good marriage'. His son married into the family of the Dean of Canterbury. Harriette, the grandmother of Dorothea Worsley-Taylor, who donated the Watkin Collection to the Chetham's Library, married into the Worsley-Taylor family of Moreton Hall, near Whalley in Lancashire. The few photographs of Harriette that have remained all show a shy but attractive lady, who always lowers her gaze as would befit a young lady in those male-dominated times. One report on Watkin the politician lists only his father and his son as the family details.

After he suffered a heart attack and resigned the chairmanship of his three major railways Watkin decided not to stand again for Parliament at the general election of 1895. His last years in the House of Commons had been sad, a long way away from the promise that Richard Cobden had seen in him when he was standing for the first time in Yarmouth in 1857. He had fought elections under several different banners: as a 'pure' Liberal, i.e. with a Tory opponent, then as he drifted to the right politically his views became close enough to the Conservatives for him to be returned unopposed. In his last years as an MP he sat as a Liberal Unionist, a Conservative in all but name and lobbied rather desperately to be made a baronet. A private exchange of correspondence shows how alienated he was by then from the Liberals since it was with Sir Philip Rose, the chief legal advisor to the Conservative party and a close friend of Disraeli, now Lord Beaconsfield and about to resign as Prime Minister for the last time. In the exchange of letters Watkin leaves no stone unturned in his pursuit of a further political honour. 'I feel sure that a communication from you to Lady Salisbury would settle it.' He reminds Sir Philip of how much work he had put into transforming Grimsby into a world fishing port.

He mentions that he (Watkin) had put up a statue to Prince Albert in Grimsby and invited the Prince of Wales (the future King Edward VII) to unveil it. The inscriptions on three sides of the statue record a visit to Grimsby by Prince Albert in 1852, his speech on that occasion and the unveiling of the statue in July 1879. The fourth side gives credit where credit was due: 'To commemorate the inauguration and completion of these great works this memorial has been erected by Sir Edward William Watkin, MP, Chairman of the Manchester, Sheffield and Lincolnshire Railway Company'.

Just to make sure he ends one letter to Sir Philip: 'I forget if I told you that the Queen accepted from me shortly after, an Album containing drawings of the Statue and an account of our doings at the unveiling – and I had a most flattering letter from Balmoral reiterating her regret that she was prevented from personally performing the ceremony.' Another letter reads: 'I have heard nothing. I know you will do all you can – and so, I must leave it. I have, as admitted, done my part, and, I do not doubt, for a moment, that a single word to the Queen from Lord B(eaconsfield), referring to the Statue at Grimsby – would – on that ground alone – be sufficient.' It ends: 'An intolerant Liberal Majority will consider me as of no use – and I shall have to join that moderate Party who before long will become absorbed in your Party. So, please, get it done.' A note by Sir Philip at the close of the file of letters from Watkin records the result of Watkin's lobbying: 'Sir Edward Watkin, who had been knighted in 1868, was created a baronet on May 12th 1880. This was one of the honours conferred on the retirement of Lord Beaconsfield from power after W Gladstone's Midlothian campaign in 1880, when the Liberals swept all before them.'

Watkin's last years brought him little pleasure. In 1892, though, an event occurred that should have brought him happiness. He married again. His second wife, Ann Ingram, was the widow of his great friend, Herbert Ingram, the founder and editor of the *Illustrated London News*, the first illustrated news magazine in the world and by far the biggest selling magazine in Britain. The two men were very similar in temperament. Magdalen Goffin, in her book *The Watkin Path*, writes: 'They shared imagination, drive, a certain ruthlessness, business ability, obstinacy, a flair for publicity and at the very end, a wife.'

In 1860 Ingram and his oldest son were drowned when their ship collided with another vessel in Lake Michigan and sank with the loss of 295 lives. Watkin took over the financial management of the paper, which was shaky, and put it on a firm footing. Thirty years later, in 1890, Ann Ingram again asked him for help. She was concerned at the way her two remaining sons, William and Charles, were running the business. She gave Watkin power of attorney and in spite of the sons' opposition Watkin represented her on the board of a new company formed to run the *News*. In a private letter to Gladstone, written in September 1890, Watkin had described Ann as 'a plain, farmer-like old lady' but, in April 1892, to the astonishment of their friends and the tittering of his enemies, Ann (80) and Edward (73) married in a service that was intended to be private, though it was held in the fashionable St George's Church in Hanover Square. An artist of the *Pall Mall Gazette* magazine was – by chance – in the church at the time. He drew some hurried sketches – the deadline for copy was 10pm the same day – and these appeared together with a report. The description of the ceremony, which lasted only 5 minutes, is rather arch. 'Sir Edward kept his eyes on the bride. She was blushing like a girl of sixteen and both the "happy pair" seemed to be enjoying suppressed amusement.' The rest of the article does not seem to have been written in a hurry since it was a point-by-point rebuttal of 'paragraphs … industriously circulated in the press … and based on the authority of members of one of the families concerned'. The 'members of one of the families' were William and Charles Ingram. William had told friends that the marriage was disgusting and if he met Watkin he would take a horsewhip to him. Charles said that the marriage was a 'public scandal'. William Ingram had already written a letter to *The Times* mocking Watkin's plans for tunnels under the English Channel and the sea between Ireland and Scotland.

Rumours were spread that Watkin had married Ann for her money. A typical article appeared in an American newspaper with little concern for accuracy. The headline sets the tone: 'Sir Edward Watkin married. The Bride a 63-year-old Widow with an Enormous Fortune.' The report concludes:

[Sir Edward] was born in 1819 and is well preserved. Mrs Ingram, her children say, is almost bedridden. Both the sons and daughters of Mrs Ingram opposed the union. Their mother had received under their father's will nearly £1,000,000. They do not hesitate to denounce Watkin as a fortune hunter. They claim that he told her that with £1,000,000 at his command he would certainly be able to gain a peerage.

The financial allegations were untrue. Watkin was a wealthy man and the second Lady Watkin's will shows that he was not a beneficiary. He had also made sure that none of Ann's money would go to his children (and none of his would go to her children either). William and Charles contested the will, alleging that their mother had been of unsound mind. They lost the case. In a letter to Gladstone written in 1894, Watkin invited the prime minister to stay with him at Mount Felix House, a splendid mansion in Walton-on-Thames, set in parkland in Surrey. He omitted to mention in the letter that the house belonged to Ann Ingram.

Watkin's two children were against the marriage, though Ann's five daughters were in favour, but it was the whiff of public ridicule that must have been most wounding. Reputation had always been important to him. Way back in 1865, during his activities in Canada, he had written to John MacDonald, soon to become the first prime minister of the new Dominion, to say how upset he was at what he called 'snubs'. The public ridicule that followed the failure of the Channel tunnel project in 1882 and the jibe of 'Watkin's Folly' had already hurt him deeply.

In 1896, after only four years of their marriage, Watkin's second wife died. His chief link with fame, Gladstone, had left office for the last time as prime minister in 1894 and died four years later. Watkin had been too ill to attend the funeral. They had been close friends. In one of fifty formal and informal letters between the two men, preserved in the Gladstone Papers in the British Library and spanning twenty-nine years, Watkin writes: 'I'll run over to Hawarden (Gladstone's castle in North Wales) and take my chance on finding you at home.' In another, he sends the prime minister 'the sample of butter I promised' and in a third, after excusing 'his scribble', he wishes Gladstone 'many happy returns of the day'. One of the last is a formal acceptance from 1894 of an invitation to a dinner at 10 Downing Street to commemorate Gladstone's retirement as prime minister at the age of 85. The social and business entries in his engagement diary, so important to him, had dried up, leaving only the consolation of the formal letters and cards of invitation saved from his and Mary's happiest years. After the brilliance of his successes, many achieved by the sheer force of his personality, there is a sadness about the last years of the once dominant Railway King. One journalist wrote: 'He dragged on for some time, a pathetic little figure, at the board meetings which he used to control in such a masterly manner. A little man, with aquiline features, he had the mouth and jaw of the born fighter.' T.S. Eliot said the way the world ends is not with a bang but a whimper. A life in the public eye that had lasted almost fifty years and had meant so much to Watkin was ending, some years before his physical life ended.

His last two domestic speeches in the House of Commons concerned the unsatisfactory state of the lavatories in the Palace Hotel in Southport. On 31 March 1892 he put down his last parliamentary question on an international matter. It concerned a proposed tunnel but this one was not under the English Channel but through the Rock of Gibraltar.

The last photograph of him, previously unpublished, shows him as an old man sitting in a chair at Rose Hill. He is well dressed and holding a walking stick. His eyes are bright but his brow is furrowed and he looks slightly puzzled, like an old bull recoiling after charging a tree unsuccessfully. It could be a metaphor for parts of his life.

On 31 March 1901 the first census of the twentieth century was taken. It recorded the names of the people residing at Rose Hill on census day. Watkin is described as 'Landed Proprietor'. Two other people listed are Marguerite Little and Jessie Mavitty, sick nurses. Fourteen days later, on 13 April, Sir Edward, who had come to his family home for the last time the previous September, died at Rose Hill. He left only £17,308 in his will, a paltry sum for someone who had earned vast sums of money at various stages of his life and who had been in modern day terms a multi-millionaire. He once told a solicitor friend that any profits he made from his railway activities went equally to his wife, his son and his daughter. Many years previously the cause of his nervous breakdown had been given as overwork. The death certificate gave the cause as 'Exhaustion'.

On 20 April he was buried next to Mary and his father and mother in the family mausoleum of St Wilfrid's Church in Northenden. One boat registered by the MSLR in Grimsby had his personal mark on it – SS *Northenden*. The day after Watkin's funeral it ran aground in the River Elbe in Germany.

Chapter 12

Beyond the Railways

References today to Edward Watkin, such as they are, focus almost exclusively on his railway achievements. This is reflected in the titles of the two published biographies, 'The Last of the Railway Kings' and 'The Second Railway King'. But in order to grasp the enormous breadth and depth of the man's work and his vision we need also to take into account the five other focus points of his career: Manchester, his work as an MP, Canada, the Channel Tunnel and the tower in London.

The significance of Watkin's involvement in the railways is reduced further in a study of the whole man by his lack of enthusiasm for trains. Yet enthusiasm was the hallmark of Watkin's character. When he took his son to visit Rose Hill for the first time, Absalom wrote: 'Edward was more desirous than ever to commence farming'. Both his father and Cobden chose the same striking word 'ardour' in descriptions of him. When Absalom took his family to see the world's first timetable passenger train arrive in Manchester in September 1830 his diary shows that he had a sense that history was being made. He had reserved places for his family on a stand next to the track and it was indeed a great occasion. The crowds at Liverpool were described by an onlooker as a 'combination of the Lord Mayor's Show and Epsom Races'. What was described as an 'unprecedented concourse' had gathered in Manchester. The day became even more dramatic when William Huskisson MP fell under the wheels of a carriage and became the world's first railway fatality.

It would be a good story, therefore, to say that from that day forward the thrill of the railways was in Edward's blood. But it is not true. There is no mention by Absalom of any excitement in his son at seeing his first railway train, even though it must have seemed like a monster to the boy, hissing steam and throwing out brilliant sparks. The day seems to have made no particular impression on Edward and he does not seem to have spoken about it in his years of public life. When Absalom went back a few days later to look at the spot where the MP had been fatally injured it was his younger son, John, not Edward, that he took with him. In the six years covered by his own diaries Watkin often mentions travelling on the railway but the references are all only factual. He sometimes went somewhere by train. Just that. No ardour. And this, it seems, is how he saw the railways for the rest of his life. His interest in trains was utilitarian, not vocational. He saw them literally and metaphorically as the means of getting somewhere, achieving his immediate or long-term aims. Even though trains made him rich and famous he seems to have had no emotional attachment to them and – unlike his son, who became a qualified engine driver – he never showed any interest in the technical and sentimental marvel of steam locomotives.

Why then did Watkin pursue a career in the railways? The answer is that he needed money. He wanted to marry Polly and to get away from his father's dominance and the dust of the warehouse. And he must have had a dawning sense of his own powers. Those sensational soirées had shown him to be capable of greater things. In 1844 the railways were where fortunes could be made – and quickly.

Polly came from a well-off family and was used to a high standard of life. That earlier quotation from his diary shows how trapped he felt at his financial situation: 'I want to marry. I am keeping a woman I love indefinitely waiting and I cannot tell when or how I must manage to furnish my house or keep my wife and myself after I am married!' Yet, on the face of it, money should not really have been a problem. His future in the family firm was assured. His father was a wealthy cotton merchant and had just made him a partner. On Absalom's death he would, as the eldest son, inherit a thriving company. But that was his dilemma. Staying in the family firm meant continuing to work in the dreary and suffocating world of Cottonopolis. He dreaded spending the rest of his life 'selling calico'. What made that prospect even more daunting was that it would mean continuing to work in the considerable shadow of his locally prominent father.

At first, the prospect of going to work for the Trent Valley Railway seemed to tick all the boxes. After writing about his fear that he would never achieve anything better in life than working for his father he reveals in the next sentence where the attraction of the railways lay: he had just made a profit on some railway shares. When he accepts the post with the

Trent Valley he adds: 'Tootal (the major shareholder in the railway) says he will make my fortune.' Only a few weeks later though he was beginning to have second thoughts about pursuing a career with the railways and his doubts centred on money. On 23 November 1845 he writes in his diary: 'When I entered upon Railway business … everything was at a premium, now discount instead of premium stands on the share list'. He refers to 'an incontinent haste to get out' and adds: 'I have lost near £1000.'

Adding to his financial doubts was the attractive prospect of an alternative career in journalism. He had written about this earlier in the year that he went to work for the Trent Valley. 'I have been busy for a project for a new newspaper.… I seem to be thought by some as the likely man to manage it.' (Working for a newspaper paralleled that offer which had been made to his father eighteen years earlier, when Absalom had been asked to become editor of the *Manchester Gazette*.) He would be joint owner with John Bright and others of the new *Manchester Examiner* and contribute articles and editorials. By the end of November he had joined Bright and two others in putting up the money for the *Examiner* to be published and by the December his doubts about continuing with his post with the Trent Valley had grown: 'I am hesitating and deliberating whether or not to give up my situation and take my chance with the paper.' Working for a small provincial railway must have tasted at times like thin gruel.

In the end, though, he decided to follow that deceptively simple but liberating maxim: 'If you're given a choice, choose both'. The newspaper was founded but he continued to work for the Trent Valley as well. Within three years, however, his *Examiner* had been merged with the *Manchester Times* and he was working for London and North Western Railway. He was now playing with the big boys. He never returned to a career in writing, though three published books, three privately printed pieces and his many fine speeches show what might have been. Cobden's judgement about his artistic talent was correct.

But even if Watkin, needing money to provide for his family, concentrated at first on working in the railways, the absence of any sense of vocation about railways and his pursuit of those five other highlights rule trains out as the linking theme to his life. For that, we must look elsewhere.

Sir Edward Elgar's famous *Enigma Variations* are portraits in music describing his wife and friends. Elgar never revealed the name of the music on which the fourteen variations are based, hence the title that the work is always known by. What he did say, however, was that over-arching all fourteen was 'another and larger theme that "goes" but is not played'. Hardly a great help but then Elgar loved puzzles.

There is a parallel here with our Sir Edward. Watkin had a lasting passion that kick-started his public career and lent coherence to a life that otherwise might seem sometimes to have darted off at random. What 'went' through all his activities even though it was not always 'played' was politics.

The finest caricaturist of the day, Carlo Pellegrini, who signed himself 'Ape', published a series of cartoons in *Vanity Fair* magazine in the 1870s under the title of 'Statesmen'. He drew all the prominent men of Victorian England and a selection from abroad. The list included Gladstone, Disraeli and the Archbishop of Canterbury. Overseas representatives included Bismarck and the Pope. In November 1875 his subject was Edward Watkin, with the caption: 'The Railway Interest'. The reference is to a phrase that Watkin often used to describe himself by, but it is incomplete. In full it was: 'A politician in the railway interest'. The failure to see Watkin as a politician is typical of descriptions of him, both in his lifetime and since.

The over-emphasis on Watkin the railwayman ignores his considerable political career. His parliamentary career spanned thirty-eight years, though because of election defeats he served as an MP for only twenty-five. He is recorded in Hansard as having made 431 speeches. That editorial in the *Manchester Guardian* just after Watkin was knighted reported: 'A short time since, Sir Edward Watkin expressed a desire to lessen his labours in connection with railway management.' A newspaper article in October 1881 put it more clearly: 'Nothing exasperates Sir Edward Watkin so much as to find himself considered purely and simply as a railway man.' Born seven weeks after the iconic political event of Peterloo, he grew up surrounded at Rose Hill by his father's world of reform politics. Absalom's political eminence, peaking in the passing of the Reform Bill and the campaign to repeal the Corn Laws, meant that visits by leading politicians to the family home and political discussion were the norm in Edward's formative years. Breaking opponents' heads in Stephenson

Square in Manchester and thrashing Chartists at public meetings must have been thrilling for a young man. They were what might be called the 'practical' side of politics in those days, when fighting was not uncommon at political gatherings. He went on to blossom and mature through his work with his father and Cobden in the Anti-Corn Law movement. His articles for the *Manchester Guardian* about the need for public parks in the town had shown he was a skilled political writer. They had even made it possible to lobby the prime minister in Downing Street. Catching the public's eye must have been exciting for someone full of energy and longing to stretch his wings.

The decade from the mid-1840s was the only period in Watkin's active life when he turned his back on political involvement. He devoted himself to his employment with the railways. However, his diary at the time contains a significant passage: 'I have not attended a single public meeting on political subjects. I have not written more than one piece of an article and have scarcely read anything. I have been almost solely a man of business…. something more than business is required.' He was still conscious of what was the mainstream of his life. That accounts for the way he flirted in 1846 with the Liberal electors of Stafford by letting them believe he could be their parliamentary candidate when he knew he was not qualified. By 1857, what Cobden had called 'the vortex of politics' had sucked him in again when he put up for MP for Yarmouth – in spite of his demanding post with the MSLR – and won. That set the pattern for the remainder of his public life, which became a balancing act between the world of politics and each of his other interests at the time. Undoubtedly the high point was played out in Canada, where he combined extraordinary political vision with the development of vast railway systems. It was a marriage made in heaven.

The decision of the directors of the failing Grand Trunk Railway of Canada to appoint Watkin to rescue the company was of course purely commercial. The company's finances were in a mess and they had found someone who could deliver, brilliantly. Watkin was delighted to accept the post for he loved a challenge, particularly one that was clearly going to involve a scrap. But behind the commercial challenge was that far more exciting political scenario, the creation of a new country. The approach by the Colonial Secretary for him to help unite Canada chimed perfectly with what Watkin had written in his magazine article, when he had promoted 'the idea of a great British nation planted for ever under the Crown and extending from the Atlantic to the Pacific'. The wellspring of that scheme was certainly not simply commercial. It was what one Canadian writer had called 'Watkin's evangelical mission', to spread what he saw as Britain's unique civilising culture across the whole of Canada. His article had continued: 'A great nation like ours cannot stand still.... A railway across [Canada] would lead to the diffusion of our civilisation and the extension of our moral empire.' In the dedication of his book *Recollections of Canada and the States* Watkin wrote of Canada as 'a great integral part of the Empire of the Queen'. He wanted his giant railway to be called the Queen Victoria Road. His description of Canada as 'large enough for large ideas' hints at his sense of frustration with the politicians of Little England.

Watkin's great scheme to dig a tunnel under the English Channel shared many of the features of his activities in Canada. It was, of course, a commercial undertaking but dominated by politics since he was directly taking on the government and the Establishment. Its failure had nothing to do with trade or railway technology. It was political. One of Watkin's most revealing speeches, made in August 1887, shows a view that would alienate many British people even today: 'While Europe is becoming more and more one country only by the piercing of mountains, the bridging over of rivers, and the breaking-down of old ideas of exclusion, we, in England, on the other hand, are becoming more and more isolated.' In a wistful comment to a Folkestone newspaper he once said: 'It is so easy on a fine afternoon to run across to France and to escape from the sense of insular confinement that seems to oppress the minds of many of our countrymen.' Such statements would be controversial in twenty-first-century Britain, with its chronic anguish over its relations with the Continent of Europe. In an age when Britain was so obviously the world's top dog they must have seemed outrageous to many people, not just to the government.

Watkin was no Little Englander. His attitude towards Europe had a parallel in his (and his father's) concern for Ireland, which in his day was just as much a part of the United Kingdom as England, Scotland and Wales. His plan for a railway tunnel between Ireland and Scotland originated in the anger (which he shared with his father) at the way the rest of Britain had ignored the poverty of Ireland. His break with his friend and supporter Gladstone came over the latter's policy to give Ireland a measure of Home Rule. Watkin saw this as abandoning part of his country. His concern for Ireland can be seen in that diary entry in 1846, when he wrote: 'I feel we have more than our share of blessings – and this at a time when trade is depressed and the Irish starving.'

Watkin remained a politician throughout his life, with many of his actions owing their origin to his political vision. But there was sometimes a dark side to his politics. Goethe, the German Shakespeare, once wrote: 'Where there is a bright light there is always a deep shadow', in other words, our strengths are our weaknesses. In Watkin's case this can be seen most dramatically in his political control for over thirty years of a town that one writer strikingly called his private bride. Grimsby.

Several obituaries commented that in Watkin's dominance of the railway scene in Britain he resembled an American railroad boss rather than an English businessman. One Australian newspaper more shrewdly said that he displayed: 'for railway directorship, management, and finance, all the genius that has been shown by the cleverest Americans.... but he also had political, social and literary capabilities such as few American millionaires have displayed'.

His delight at being in charge was never more evident than in the way he ran Grimsby as a kind of fiefdom. It had more than a whiff about it of what was called in America 'Tammany Hall' politics, after the ruthless organisation that ran Democratic politics in New York in the second half of the nineteenth century. The head of Tammany Hall was William M. Tweed, known as 'Boss' Tweed. His machine was highly efficient and based on patronage. Watkin's Grimsby had uncomfortable parallels with it.

It is often said that Watkin's creation of Grimsby was due to his introduction of a new railway. In an article in 1979 one local paper said: 'Before Sir Edward's railway, a village; afterwards, a Victorian boom town.' In fact, the MSLR had reached the Lincolnshire port some years before Watkin took over as chairman but its early trade had been mainly in coal and timber. In 1857 there were only twenty-two boats in Grimsby and in the whole of 1861 the port handled only 5,300 tons of fish. Watkin's genius, as with the Met, was in identifying potential. He persuaded three other railway companies to join with the MSLR to form the Grimsby Deep Sea Fishing Company and the town was soon putting fish on the tables of all the great cities of the North and the Midlands as well as London. Grimsby's fame did not stop there, however. In 1880 one railway historian, having called Grimsby the 'great fish shop of England', continued: 'It is just possible that England is responsible for the growing military spirit in Germany for there is nothing so exhilarating as phosphorous and it is a fact that the best tables in Berlin are graced with Grimsby fish.'

By the end of his reign over Grimsby the fish tonnage had doubled and doubled again and more, and Watkin had developed it into the largest fishing port in the world. Probably for the last time in the history of Great Britain workers from the South of England came in their thousands to work up north, in Watkin's new fish dock. But his plans for the port did not stop at fish. He developed its trade in grain and coal and set up passenger routes to Hamburg, Rotterdam and St Petersburg. The skipper of one of the company's boats at Grimsby was present at the opening of the new Royal Dock and commented: 'It's not big enough for Sir Edward.... If truth were known, he'd like to make a dock of the North Sea and put a goods warehouse on the Dogger Bank.' With his usual flair for publicity he invited the Prince and Princess of Wales to open a canal link between two Grimsby docks in 1879 and arranged for a statue of Prince Albert to be erected outside the newly named Royal Hotel.

For more than thirty years Watkin exercised a not always benevolent dictatorship over Grimsby – he boasted that he had made the fortune of everyone in the town. All Grimsby's MPs had either a close connection to his railway or were even employed by it. They did as they were told by the MSLR, or more particularly by Watkin, who in essence selected them. It is an irony that the Grimsby parliamentary constituency had in effect become one of the rotten boroughs that Absalom had fought so hard to abolish in the Reform Act of 1832.

The quality of the town's MPs was awful. Colonel George Tomline was said to be the wealthiest commoner in England and the worst MP in Parliament. He was rarely seen in the House of Commons. In his six years in the House he figured in Hansard only twenty-two times. The local joke during his time was that Grimsby was the only large town that had no MP. Henri Josse MP was a political exile from France and made his fortune as a coal merchant in Grimsby. He was a member of the town council and a magistrate as well as an MP, even though his spoken English was difficult to understand. He was totally loyal to the railway and Edward Watkin personally. He once wrote: 'I believe in the enterprising genius of Sir Edward Watkin. It may be doubted whether any man has conferred greater or more signal benefit on any town than the chairman of the MSLR on Grimsby.'

In August 1877 Grimsby politics erupted dramatically. The occasion was a parliamentary by-election and the night the result was declared became known as the Royal Hotel Riot. The winner – as always in Grimsby – was the Liberal candidate but he was, even for Grimsby, totally unsuitable to be an MP. He had only one qualification: he was Edward's son, Alfred. Even the *Illustrated London News* (founded by Watkin's friend, Herbert Ingram) sounded distinctly underwhelmed in its description of the new MP: 'Mr Watkin is thirty or thirty-one years of age. He has devoted himself to practical engineering and has achieved some reputation in that department. He is married to a daughter of the Dean of Canterbury. He has not yet taken any active part in political public life.' Another description of Alfred was more scathing. It dismissed him as 'somewhat dim and very deaf'.

Election days in the nineteenth century were almost like a bank holiday. There was always plenty to drink as groups of excited supporters roamed the constituency, whipping the votes in. Watkin had made sure that his son had enough money to ferry voters from outlying districts and this caused bad blood among his opponents since there was a suspicion that not all of them were entitled to vote in Grimsby.

The campaign was bitter and brought out all of Watkin's aggression, made even sharper because he was fighting for his son. He had never been a stranger to the libel courts and when a rumour was put about that his successes in Canada had involved some shady financial deals he went on the attack. He published a poster from the Royal Hotel, where he was staying during the campaign. It offered a £50 reward (the equivalent of £6,000 today) for anyone who could give him the name of the member of the Tory committee who had 'circulated a FALSE AND SCANDALOUS ATTACK' on him. The poster ended: 'I add that the man NELSON, whose name is used, IS A RASCAL, he having obtained £100 from me some years ago for expenses of a journey in America which he never performed.'

The polling day result created uproar. Alfred Watkin had 1,699 votes and the runner-up 1,315. But the record showed that the popular third candidate had received only 97 votes. After the count the mood turned ugly and a mob, reported in the *Liverpool Daily Post* as 6,000-strong, marched on the Royal Hotel, where Alfred, who found difficulty in stringing two words together, tried to make a speech from the hotel balcony. He was hissed and booed and a group stormed the hotel. All the doors had been locked so the men plundered a coal train to set fire to the hotel and used timber from the nearby docks as battering rams. Inside the hotel the supporters of the new MP had armed themselves with stair rods, pokers, fire irons and a pair of pistols. One enterprising man opened a book on how long the new MP would last. The mob captured a downstairs refreshment room and downed 30 gallons of beer, a barrel of whisky and half a barrel of port. The local police arrived but when they realised that they were outnumbered, they wisely stood back and took notes. Several people and policemen were injured by flying stones, one of which is still on show in the town museum. By midnight the battle was still raging so it was decided to call in the army from Sheffield. They did not arrive till 6am, 4 hours after the mob had gone home, apart from a couple of drunks asleep on the pavement outside the hotel. The *Grimsby Observer* later pointed out that there were more people involved in the fight than had been involved in the election.

Watkin, keen to have the last word on the matter, put down a question in Parliament. After stating that the recent election at Grimsby was 'thoroughly peaceful and good-humoured ... until four hours after the close of the poll', he asked 'whether it was not the opinion of the authorities of Grimsby that the disturbances were promoted by foreign agencies, and if one of the foreign agents was not a gentleman who gave the name of Lamb, and who is assumed to be one of the well-known Lamb family of Nottingham'.

Alfred Watkin did not stand for re-election. His political career had lasted only three years.

The Grimsby story does, however, have one positive outcome. Just 2 miles further along the coast was a small fishing village called Cleethorpes. In 1863 Watkin extended the railway to Cleethorpes to provide a seaside outlet for the thousands of new workers in his enormous port. When a private company built a pier Watkin had another of his visions: he realised the potential of Cleethorpes as a holiday resort not only for his workers but for the citizens of Sheffield and Nottingham. He acquired land next to the sea and built pleasure gardens and a swimming pool on it then bought the private pier and extended it. Every winter storms would erode the cliffs next to the village so in 1880 the MSLR paid for a new mile-long defensive sea wall to be built. (It incorporated a folly, which is still called Ross Castle, named after a former secretary of the MSLR.) In 1892 the company bought the remaining 33 acres of land along the front between Grimsby and Cleethorpes. In all they spent £100,000 (equivalent to nearly £1 million pounds today) on the development of the little village and by the end of the century Cleethorpes had become a major holiday resort. On a single day in 1890 it had 30,000 visitors.

Grimsby and Cleethorpes were highly profitable winners for 'Boss' Watkin. A grateful Town Council gave him the freedom of Grimsby in 1891. But his achievements in Grimsby are a dark example of his single-minded determination to pursue an aim, though their unattractive details should not be exaggerated. He did after all re-create the town and its satellite, providing employment for thousands of people.

Even if Watkin's aggressiveness must have often led beaten opponents to look for some dirty linen to wash in public, it is significant that his public life was free of scandal. Only he and George Hudson have ever been called Railway Kings and they certainly had a great deal in common. One writer drew detailed parallels between the two men but highlighted one difference:

> [Watkin] might, in fact, be compared with Hudson in many respects, in his power of persuasion, in his grasp of finance, his intimacy with railway problems, his organising skill and appreciation of able officers, in his far-seeing estimates of future development – above all, in the great ambition that distracted him and led to wasteful struggles and unnecessary promotions. But, unlike Hudson, he was honest.

Hudson had to flee abroad to avoid arrest.

A cynical view might be that it was perhaps because he was honest that Watkin did not succeed as a politician. Another may be that his inner compulsion meant that he never stopped looking for that final success which was always just round the corner and that this restlessness was the cause of his tangents, that itch that could never be scratched to his satisfaction. Although he developed or created scores of railways, like his father he never found a home in the straitjacket and compromises of party politics.

Chapter 13

The House that Came Back from the Dead

The close of a long and eventful life on 13 April 1901 does not mark the end of the Watkin story. It has two further twists to it, both centring on the family home, Rose Hill. The first involves the rescue of the house after ten years of decay, when it was about to collapse. The second is an intriguing detective story of the twentieth-century art world, with a trail that started with Edward Watkin and led from Rose Hill to the Dallas Museum of Art in Texas, taking in the United States' top auction house, Sotheby's of New York, on the way. That twist could be called 'Watkin's Last Laugh'.

What remains of Rose Hill House – the family home for sixty-eight years from 1834 – is one of only a few surviving physical links with the Watkin story. However, its importance extends way beyond the family since in both Absalom's and Edward's days it had welcomed as guests some of the most eminent people in Britain. That is why it has been awarded the coveted Grade II* listed building national classification. This special status makes it all the more shocking that at the opening of the twenty-first century Rose Hill came close to total collapse.

If you travel across northern Germany you pass through a succession of exquisite half-timbered mediaeval towns and villages, each with its own ancient marketplace and houses decorated with pious mottoes carved in the wooden beams of the lintels of ancient doors. But this is the Central European Plain, where the Allied tanks destroyed the German Army on their way to Berlin in 1944 and 1945. They razed most of the towns in their path as well, en passant. In the 1950s, as Germany began to recover from the devastation of war, the villages and small towns set about restoring their centres to what they had been. The work was carried out with great skill and it is hard to credit that most of the buildings you see nowadays are only seventy years old, beautiful but copies.

And that is what Rose Hill House is today, a beautiful copy. Its manicured grounds set it apart from the twenty-first-century houses built round it on the lands that were formerly owned by Absalom and Edward Watkin. Its front entrance has a solid nineteenth-century door with a biblical text in Latin in the fanlight: 'Nisi dominus frustra' – in full 'Except the Lord build the house, they labour in vain that build it'. But the Lord did not build most of what you see. That was the work of skilled architects and craftsmen in 2003. They did a brilliant job for when they started Rose Hill was derelict and vandalised. Its roof was leaking, dry and wet rot were everywhere, the beautiful stained glass windows installed by Edward and his wife had been smashed, their magnificent copper fireplace in the entrance hall had been stolen for the value of its metal and the elaborately carved staircase had been set on fire.

This is the first time that the full story of one of England's most historic houses has been told. Its rise and fall and rise again spans more than 200 years. Starting out as a farmhouse in the late eighteenth century, by the second half of the nineteenth century it had become an opulent mansion where all those famous people stayed as guests and walked round its magnificent gardens and woods after dinner. That was its golden age. It was to be followed by ninety years of gentle decline and then its darkest decade, the 1990s.

When Absalom Watkin bought Rose Hill in 1832 he described it in his diary as 'an ill-contrived, cottage-looking house with a barn and a stable', though a week later it was 'larger than I thought and will need very little addition'. In October 1833, some months before the family moved to Northenden, Absalom brought in builders and a landscape gardener but after that initial burst of enthusiasm he seems to have had little interest in the house. The only other references to it in his diaries are his complaints at his wife's inability to keep it clean.

In Absalom's day Rose Hill had only two reception rooms, and when guests came to stay they slept in the main bedroom, while the Watkin family doubled up in the smaller bedrooms. Until he built a cottage for the gardener and his wife all the 'outside staff' lived off-site. By 1839 the tithe map shows Absalom as the owner of six parcels of land surrounding his house, which for the first time carries the name 'Rose Hill'. Access to the estate was from the back via Shawcross Lane, an ancient road leading from the church, but in 1840 Absalom bought another two fields and built a new road connecting the house to Longley Lane. It cost him £340, at today's prices £20,000. That is the last mention in Absalom's diaries of any structural improvements to the estate. From now on the only references to his property are to the beauty of his land, his gardens and his trees. On the first day of May 1853 he planted some copper beech trees in the wood in front of the house. They are still there, as are the outlines of the paths he created.

When Absalom died on 16 December 1861 Rose Hill and its lands passed to Edward as his oldest son and its greatest years began. By then Edward was a figure of national, soon to be international, importance. The year in which his father died was when he was asked by the Colonial Secretary to go to British North America to take part in negotiations to create a new country, Canada. The following year he became the president of the Grand Trunk Railway in Canada and in 1864 he was elected MP for Stockport. He needed an impressive house and estate where he could entertain people of influence in the worlds of business, politics and the arts. He and his wife set about transforming Rose Hill, though, as we have seen, the main credit for its development was Mary's.

No photographs or paintings of the house as it was in Edward's lifetime have survived so we have to rely on later images and secondary sources to get some idea of how Rose Hill looked in its greatest years. An aerial photo taken in 1929, twenty-eight years after Edward's death, shows how extensive the Watkin estate and gardens had become. A letter written in the same year refers to 13 acres of gardens and lawns and 37 acres of land under arable cultivation. It describes Rose Hill as 'a villa'.

You entered through the fine porch with its biblical quotation in the stained glass over the door. The glass matched the lovely designs in the windows to the left and right of the entrance. The magnificent entrance hall, which was also the main reception area, was the jewel in the crown.

It was ornately decorated and finished with William Morris wallpaper. Your eye was taken by the beautiful scrolled copper fireplace with its fine oak-panelled surround, and the richly carved staircase. To your left was the ballroom. In addition to the picture gallery, several reception rooms and Absalom's library on the ground floor, the hall opened by means of a six-panelled door onto the drawing room, which had a ceiling embellished with an elaborate stencilled decoration in gold and red with a central floral medallion. The large dining room opened out onto what had been Absalom's pride and joy, his walled garden, and along a short corridor on the other side of the dining room was the billiard room, to which the men could retire after dinner. It was decorated with manly sketches of royalty including the then Duke of Edinburgh, members of Edward's London club, the Marlborough, and other celebrities of the time. There was also a facility that was seen by the second half of the nineteenth century as an essential provision next to a billiard room, a lavatory, in the previous century usually called the 'necessary' but in our times softened to the less urgent 'convenience'.

Improved necessaries were one of mid-nineteenth-century Britain's most welcome inventions. A London plumber called Thomas Crapper invented the ballcock, which made flush toilets possible, although – contrary to popular opinion – he did not, unlike William Henry Hoover, add a new verb to the English language. Absalom perhaps shared Crapper's interest in necessaries. Some years ago a triangular stone bearing the word 'Stercoracium' was found in the woods next to the house. It is something of a mystery. 'Stercoracium' is a made-up, jokey Latin-sounding word, meaning lavatory, necessary or convenience. What is slightly odd about the stone, which is a coping stone, is that it was important enough to have chiselled into it the initials AW and the date 1858, three years before Absalom died. Perhaps Absalom built a necessary in his grounds and was so pleased with it that he decided to sign it.

On 26 September 1887 Sir Edward and Lady Watkin invited 400 local children and their teachers to Rose Hill to celebrate his 68th birthday. The occasion was described in a local paper as 'most pleasant and right royal'. (The last adjective would have particularly pleased the Watkins.) The following January a ball was held to celebrate Lady Watkin's 64th birthday. Both occasions were described, respectfully, in the local papers, the *Stockport Advertiser* (since Rose Hill was in Cheshire in those days Stockport was the nearest town) and the *(Cheshire) County News and Chronicle*. One feature of both afternoons was tours of the house for the admiring guests – and reporters, who knew their place. Their accounts are unique since they provide the only surviving contemporary descriptions of Rose Hill in its pomp. Both are written in language as ornate as the furnishings and they give a forelock-tugging picture of the ostentatious wealth of a man secure in his place in local and by then national society.

The *Advertiser*'s reporter wrote:

In the capacious entrance hall were striking portraits of Sir Edward and Lady Watkin, painted by Sir Frederick Grant, which (as an inscription upon one of the many silver salvers that adorned a sideboard in the dining room subsequently afforded us the information) were presented to Sir Edward, along with the salver referred to, in the year 1870 'in recognition of his very valuable service to the commercial and industrial community', whilst among the many novelties in the hall a model American car afforded a major share of interest. Rich and chaste as were the salvers mentioned they sank into insignificance when compared with the costly gold dessert service and old gold plates, the wealth in this channel being further augmented by presents displayed in several other parts of the house, not the least noticeable of which was an elegant vase (upon an ornamental pedestal), which a silver plate on its base states was 'Presented to Sir Edward Watkin MP by Count Munster, the ambassador, on behalf of the Emperor of Germany'. This, with other striking objects of interest, finds a place in the picture gallery, a room which to all intents and purposes merits the name, its walls containing some striking examples of the accomplishments of the great masters. Various pieces of sculpture and photographs lend variety and attraction to the room, the most noticeable perhaps being the striking likeness of Sir Edward and his lady, whilst in the photographic specimens Sir Edward, Lady Watkin, and their daughter, Mrs Worsley, attired in court presentation dress, afforded equal grounds for admiration. Words would fail us in attempting any detailed description of the chastely furnished morning and drawing-rooms but three paintings on the walls of the dining room call for special attention. Passing through the grandly stocked library we were introduced to the billiard room with the caricature portraits of the Marlborough Club. Exigencies of space will not permit us to enter into a description of the gardens and the grounds but we could not fail to notice the excellence of the painting and decorative processes to which the mansion throughout has been recently subjected.

The second report in the *Advertiser* says: 'The mansion and grounds generally were thrown open to the visitors, who greatly enjoyed inspecting the pictures, statuary, and plate, a large portion of the latter having been presented to the owner for public services.' As a souvenir of the day the

436 children present were each given a jubilee sixpence by Lady Watkin (it was the fiftieth year of Queen Victoria's accession to the throne). 'The recipients entered the house by the door near the conservatory, and filed through the hall, the picture gallery, and the dining room, Lady Watkin making the presentation in the latter room, the youngsters passing out through the front door.'

In its report on Lady Watkin's birthday celebrations four months later the *Advertiser* writes:

> During the evening the capacious and elegantly furnished rooms of the mansion were thrown open to the inspection of the visitors. These have been so recently described in the Advertiser that it is not necessary to recapitulate the costly and recherché contents. We may however state that since our visit, there have been one or two important additions. These comprise an ebony table which forms a case for the family jewels, which include, amongst other articles, a silver Elizabethan tea pot, a gold snuff box studded with diamonds, presented to Sir Edward, his clasp and gold medal of the Greek order, several costly brooches, a present from the Empress Eugenie, &c. Upon the table, which is beautifully finished, is engraved the family arms, with the motto 'Saie and Doe' [say and do], whilst another contribution to the wealth of the room is discovered in a silver mounted box under a glass case containing the freedom of the borough of Hythe, with which Sir Edward was lately presented, and which town it will be remembered he has represented in Parliament for a number of years. Last, though not least, either in point of attraction to the picture gallery or to the value of the additions, must be added an oil painting of Lady Watkin in Court dress – a striking likeness to the medallion family portraits, which include Sir Edward's mother and members of the family down to the fourth generation.

The contents of the 'mansion' of Rose Hill were sumptuous. One rather catty writer said, when he was looking back on the life of Edward Watkin, that Rose Hill contained: 'all that the Exhibitions of 1851 and 1862 could inspire and money could buy'. The hint that Watkin was a philistine is unfair. The art gallery at Rose Hill was his and his wife's innovation, not Absalom's. Even the billiard room was 'studded with works of art', which, according to a newspaper report, were much admired by the prime minister, Mr Gladstone, on one of his many visits to Rose Hill. Watkin extended his father's library from 2,000 to 3,000 volumes. The Watkin archive at the Chetham's Library contains a number of pencil sketches by him, including a self-portrait. As has already been mentioned, he had a fluent written style and one of his books sold out on the day it was published. An article in one New York newspaper describes him as a linguist and a *littérateur*. His second diary contains several pages of quotations from German literature.

The open afternoon to celebrate Watkin's birthday in 1887 led to further but less respectful press coverage in the *County News and Chronicle*:

> A number of the Wesleyan School children were excluded from participating in the fete by the officious, and we might say, bigoted action of someone connected with the proceedings. During the week it has been freely asserted in the village that the rector is responsible for attempting to limit the festivities to Church school children, but we cannot say if this is correct or not.

Watkin had put the detailed arrangements in the hands of the rector. The newspaper report went on: 'We ... learn that it was Sir Edward Watkin's wish that all the school children of the village should participate in the rejoicings, irrespective of sect', and a letter to the editor said: 'Owing to Sir Edward's liberal and broad unsectarian views, those Wesleyan scholars who were not present are to be presented with a Jubilee sixpence at their own schoolroom on Sunday next.'

There is only one other report of celebrations at Rose Hill. It appeared in the *Advertiser* in July 1897 and acknowledged the generosity of Sir Edward in making the grounds of the mansion available to the villagers to celebrate Queen Victoria's Diamond Jubilee. It was another splendid occasion, mirroring the birthday celebrations of ten years before, but with two differences. Lady Watkin had died and Sir Edward was by then in poor health and unable to be present.

Edward's death in 1901 marked the close of the Watkin connection with the house, though his son inherited it briefly before selling it off. Sir Alfred Watkin had no interest in Rose Hill. When Northenden celebrated the coronation of Edward VII in August 1902, the house was not host to the village ox-roast, as it would have done in Sir Edward's day. In the November the *Manchester Courier and Lancashire General Advertiser* carried an announcement:

Capes, Dunn and Pilcher have been favoured with instructions from the Executors of the late Sir Edward Watkin, Bart, to SELL BY AUCTION on Wednesday November 19, and following days, at half past 11 o'clock prompt each day, at Rose Hill, Northenden, near Manchester, the Highly Valuable HOUSEHOLD FURNITURE, Objects of Art, Pictures, Books, Billiard Table, Plate, and other Contents of the Residence. Catalogues (price 6d. each, to admit two.)

In fact, there was only one executor of Edward's will, Alfred. It was his decision to have a car boot sale of his father's and grandfather's possessions and to let people pick over the contents of historic Rose Hill, including the enormous library, at 6*d.* a time, two for the price of one.

Soon the house and its grounds too had been sold, to a Derbyshire businessman, Mr William Parkyn. In Sir Edward's day there had often been references in the Manchester papers to trips organised by the teachers of schools in the poorer areas of Manchester to Rose Hill, especially at Whitsuntide, but these ceased with his death. Clearly Mr Parkyn did not see himself as the local squire in the tradition of Sir Edward. He figures only once in the Rose Hill story, though that sole entry was to have sensational consequences, as we shall see.

In 1915 Mr Parkyn sold the house and its grounds to the Guardians of the Manchester Union and retired to Buxton. Boards of Guardians were responsible through the workhouses for the support of the poorest families in Britain under the provisions of the same Poor Law which Absalom had fought to have extended to Ireland. The Board opened Rose Hill as a hospital for children suffering from ophthalmia, an infectious eye disease brought on by the poor living conditions in the slums of central Manchester.

No formal records or photographs of the hospital have survived but two newspaper articles give a glimpse of the house and its setting at the start of the twentieth century. The first appeared in the *Manchester Courier* on 4 September 1915, to coincide with the opening of the hospital the following Thursday by the Lord Mayor of Manchester.

The building and surrounding land, 13 acres in extent, at one time belonged to the Watkin family and have been purchased by the Guardians of the Manchester Union for £7200. Sir Edward Watkin, the railway magnate, was the last member of the family to live here.

Situated in Rose Hill – the inhabitants call it Primrose Hill because of the wonderful wealth of primroses to be seen there in the spring – it is indeed a lovely spot. Those who designed the building and adornment of the house had a fine artistic taste. Oak, cunningly carved, is largely used in the interior and windows everywhere are of stained glass, the designs being of flowers, blue or red. Very noble and impressive is the entrance hall, panelled throughout in oak, with oaken arches and staircase, and beautifully wrought frieze, and wonderful fireplace. From the terrace of the house one looks out on a fair scene. The immediately surrounding country is well-wooded, and in the spring especially, when there is a positive riot of rhododendrons here, the picture is one to capture the most unimpressionable spirit. In the grounds are lovely flower gardens, a kitchen garden and an orchard, over whose walls in these days the ruddy apples hang temptingly. Truly a haunt of 'ancient peace'. The old dining hall and library will be used as schoolrooms – both are oak-panelled and beautifully appointed – and one of the large rooms of the house is to be converted into a church. Probably no Union in the Kingdom has an institution of the kind more beautiful and better equipped than this Ophthalmia School, at which are to be treated and educated children of the very poorest class.

The second article appeared in the *Manchester City News* on 1 April 1916 and describes the hospital as the only one of its kind in the North of England. The writer is enchanted by a choir of childish voices, made up of singers:

… drawn from their grey pent-up homes in the heart of the city to the old leafy haven of the Watkin family. The pleasure is enhanced by a glance round the lordly domain whose former residents loomed so large on the pages of our local annals. A gentle green slope within the grounds is beautified with purple crocuses. Nearby is a beech tree, and against it a thick low oblong stone, lettered on its four sides. On the front is the inscription: 'Absalom Watkin, born 1787, married November 3 1814, died December 16, 1861, aged seventy-four years.' On a lawn beyond a great clump of rhododendrons stands a huge rocky boulder poised on a low trunk-like pedestal. It would be interesting to know whence this giant came.

The stone commemorating Absalom was erected by Edward a year after his father's death. It has survived in its original position, though until recently it was 'lost' in the undergrowth of Rose Hill Woods. The 'huge rocky boulder', the Sharstone, was placed there by Edward after it was discovered on one of his Wythenshawe farms. The *Transactions of the Manchester Geological Society* on 9 December 1890 contained a report on what they called 'The Cheshire Boulder':

> Mr. Stirrup (Honorary Secretary) exhibited a photograph of the large boulder now lying in a field near the road leading from Ringway to Northenden, and read the following communication: **Large Boulder near Ringway**. This boulder lies at the margin of a field close to the road from Northenden to Ringway, about half a mile from Ringway Church. It is at the present time being cleared from the surrounding soil, previous to conveyance to Sir Edward Watkin's grounds at Northenden. The boulder … is a hard volcanic rock…. and has probably come from the Lake District, borne to its present place by ice.

In 1930 Boards of Guardians were abolished and their responsibilities were taken over by local councils. Rose Hill, now owned by Manchester City Council, continued as a convalescent home for children. During the Second World War it was briefly a home for unmarried mothers and their children and after the war it became a residential nursery. In 1955 it took on its final role as a public building when it became a remand home for young offenders. The boys in their green uniforms were only seen locally as they went in procession to the local churches on Sunday mornings. (That was the peak time for absconding.) The remand home was seen locally as a kind of prison. Naughty children in Northenden were told by their parents that if they did not behave they would be sent to Rose Hill.

By the close of the 1980s, however, national policies for the rehabilitation of young people were changing. Punishment was being seen not only as ineffective but counter-productive. The tide had gone out on institutions like Rose Hill and seventy-five years of use as a public building ended on 12 May 1990, when the remand home closed. By the summer the house was locked and empty, its future uncertain while its owner, Manchester City Council, investigated alternative uses.

Within a few months, however, interest in the building was being shown from outside the city. It was not far short of a hundred years since Edward Watkin's death, but Rose Hill was still recognisably his mansion. Early in 1991 it received an official visit from the grandly named Royal Commission on the Historical Monuments of England. The Commission's terms of reference were 'to compile and publish an inventory of all ancient and historical monuments in England' but it also had the power to classify structures as listed buildings because of their architectural or historical merit. On 11 April 1991 the Royal Commission awarded Rose Hill the status of Grade II*.

To be entered in the national catalogue as 'listed', buildings have to be 'nationally important and of special interest' but those which are given a star go beyond that. They are defined as 'particularly important buildings of more than special interest' and must 'illustrate important aspects of England's social, economic, cultural or military history or have close historical associations with nationally important people'. Rose Hill's star was well earned because of its association with Edward and Absalom as well as with Disraeli, Lord Salisbury, John Bright, Richard Cobden and above all with Gladstone, who was a frequent visitor. In Manchester the former home of the Watkin family joined other starred buildings such as the Midland Hotel, the Central Library and, surprisingly, Northenden Bus Depot, chosen because of its pioneering enormous concrete central arch, one of only two such structures in the whole world when it was built in 1942. (Its rival, in Berlin, was bombed by the British in the war, leaving the Northenden Depot as unique at the time.)

The Royal Commission's official listing of 1991 describes the lavish interior of Rose Hill. In view of what was about to happen to the house and its contents its elegant and specialised language is an epitaph for the grandeur of Sir Edward's mansion:

> The principal feature is the very fine quality entrance and staircase hall in the c1900 extension, with panelling, applied canvas frieze above, painted or stencilled with swags and Renaissance details, and moulded ceiling. Elaborate fireplace with beaten copper hood and back panel with art nouveau repousse decoration. The windows and doors all have very fine and imaginative art nouveau stained glass, with rose trees, birds and other flowers and plants and employing

clear glass as part of the design. The hall leads through triple-arcade to staircase with elaborately carved wooden balustrade: an art nouveau version of a Carolean stair. Interior includes further ceiling decoration in wood or plaster, including that in the chapel, and an elaborately carved mid C19 marble fireplace in the drawing room. Further stained glass in the heads of the two bay windows over the entrance hall, and in windows on left side.

Sadly, the national star classification was to cut no ice. Within ten years every one of the features listed in the report had rotted or been stolen, smashed or set on fire. The details of how this happened are revealed in a special report published by the Royal Commission in 1996 – five years after their first visit – and in correspondence revealed under the Freedom of Information Act by English Heritage, the successor to the Royal Commission.

In March 1993 Manchester decided that the land was 'surplus to the Council's requirements' and sold it for private house building. The sale did not include the woods planted by Absalom in front of the house. These remain in Council ownership as a public open space. After two further visits to Rose Hill, in 1993 and 1996, the Royal Commission decided to publish one of their rare special reports. It described the building as having been created by Sir Edward Watkin to provide 'a fit setting in which to entertain national political figures, businessmen, and members of England's literary and artistic establishment'. It included a commentary on the history and condition of the various rooms and twelve photographs of the house and grounds. What makes it a particularly valuable document is that the interval of three years between the two visits by the Commission enabled its specialists to describe in detail what had happened to Rose Hill during that period. Apart from the destruction of the stained glass windows and the carved staircase the report detailed the changes of the previous five years:

Between 1992 and 1996 the house was empty, during which time it suffered severely from theft and vandalism; a chimney piece of white marble and its surround (stolen); massive copper panel incorporating a fire hood (stolen); square stone pillar with the legend: 'God is love …' (removed); Greenhouse, Stable, Kitchen gardens (demolished); two nineteenth century lodges, ruinous in 1993 after recent fire damage and demolished by 1996; the remains of extensive kitchen gardens, constructed by Absalom Watkin (demolished).

As with the listing of Rose Hill in 1991, the special report of 1996 was ignored by the City Ccouncil and the housing company, even though it had been written by a national authority. The deterioration of the once-grand house and its surroundings continued, and one incident had an element of farce about it. The rector of St Wilfrid's Church was walking up the cobbled lane at the back of Rose Hill (the original road to the house from St Wilfrid's). He was wanting to look at Edward's memorial stone to Absalom. He realised that somebody had stolen some of the cobblestones and saw a van parked at the side of the lane. A security guard saw the rector and assumed he was one of the thieves, come back to finish the job. The guard attempted to arrest the rector, who tried to tell him who he was. There was, in the gentle words of the rector, 'a breakdown in communication' between them and they both began to shout. This attracted the attention of a second guard, who believed the rector's story and released him. The thieves and the cobblestones were never found. There is no record during a decade of vandalism and theft of anyone being apprehended at Rose Hill or brought to trial.

The sad story of Rose Hill's decline continued into the twenty-first century. In June 2001 a letter from the Northenden Civic Society to English Heritage described the house as 'a forlorn ruin'.

But January 2002 ushered in a complete change of policy by the company that had bought the house. They commissioned a firm of top-class architects and craftsmen to reconstruct what had been lost since 1994. These used the photographs taken in 1996 by the Royal Commission and what they could rescue of the original wood carving, plaster and wallpaper from inside the building. Within two years the new tenants of the reborn Rose Hill had moved in.

The advertisements in 1994 for the new houses of 'Watkin's Wood' had referred to 'this impressive and historic estate, where the Great House still stands'. Today, however, there is little sense of history about Rose Hill. The former Watkin lands are a housing estate. Only that electricity sub-station in front of the house reminds the visitor of the name 'Rose Hill', where one of the Railway Kings of the nineteenth century lived for sixty-seven years and died here. The name of the house has been replaced by a bland, upmarket and – in Nikolaus Pevsner's words – pointless title: 'Ashley Grange'. An advertisement in February 2012 for one of the apartments at Rose Hill described the house as having been lived in by the 'Absell and Watkin' family. Absalom would have smiled at that and made an appropriate entry in his diary.

What happened to Rose Hill is typical of the fate of many grand buildings in Britain, not just in Manchester. Against the background of the collapse or demolition of other fine Victorian structures, however, the sad history of Rose Hill has two redeeming features. The external structure of the house has survived and its restoration after a decade of neglect was of the highest quality. The result is that the exterior of the Watkin villa is virtually unchanged, though the outhouses and stables are gone, and three apartment blocks have replaced Absalom's Victorian garden. Internally, luxury private apartments have replaced Edward's ballroom and art gallery and Absalom's library, but the entrance hall is still spacious. It lacks the original beautiful William Morris wallpaper and the intricate plasterwork of the ceiling but new stained glass windows, a replacement copper fireplace and the sweep of the restored staircase are all impressive.

The imposing stone entrance is original, the fanlight still declares *Nisi Dominus Frustra* and it is just possible to imagine prime ministers and other notable personages of the nineteenth century coming through this door, to be received by their host and hostess, Sir Edward and Lady Mary Watkin.

Chapter 14

The Last Laugh of the Railway King

The remaining chapter in Rose Hill's history would take some beating for drama. It involves millions of pounds and has a whiff of double-dealing about it.

The story opens with William Parkyn, that Derbyshire businessman who bought the house and its grounds from Edward Watkin's son in 1902. When he sold the house on his retirement to Buxton in 1915, he decided to withdraw from the sale an enormous old painting that had been hanging at the top of the staircase in the entrance hall. Sir Edward's son had tried to sell it in 1902, when it was listed in the catalogues for auction, but it had failed to find a buyer. The St Wilfrid's parish magazine recorded in its April 1915 edition what happened next.

> The inhabitants of Northenden … have been enabled to obtain possession 'in perpetium' [sic] of a valuable work of art. It consists of a painting of great merit, depicting an Ice Field. The picture, which is large in size and handsomely mounted, has been presented by Mr Parkyn to the Northenden Church Room, and will, we are sure, be much appreciated and admired by all who see it.

The donation was intended to celebrate the opening of the new church rooms, now a supermarket car park. The announcement in the magazine was low key, printed just above a report that the Northenden Home Comforts Branch of the British Red Cross, whose aim was to provide materials for the soldiers of the First World War, were 'maintaining their enthusiasm'. Mrs Travis had 'realised £2.10s from the sale of cloth, and Miss Travis' gift of a parcel of knitted woollen goods had materially added to the stock ready'.

Although the sale of the house was not completed till the September, it is clear from a reference to Mr Parkyn as being 'late of Rose Hill' that he had already gone. His was an odd choice of gift but Mr Parkyn presumably thought the painting, though large, was of no great value. He would not be the only one who thought that over the next sixty-four years.

The painting was enormous, 5ft by 10ft, and with its heavy frame weighed in the region of 500lb. However, it proved something of an embarrassment to the church since nobody really wanted it. For six years from 1915 it hung at the back of the tiny stage in the parish rooms, usually hidden behind the curtains. Then in 1921 the Northenden Amateur Dramatic Society complained to the rector. They were putting on Shakespeare's *As You Like It* and the painting was getting in the way of the scenery. Although Mr Parkyn had long since left for the Derbyshire hills, it must have been a ticklish problem for the rector to look such a gift horse in the mouth, but he hit upon a tactful solution. The painting should return to its original home, Rose Hill, which was now a hospital owned by Manchester City Council. So the painting went back home, was hung on a landing at the top of the main staircase – and forgotten. In the next fifty-eight years the people living in Rose Hill were all just passing through; nobody was interested in an old canvas, now darkened with age. All that changed in 1979, when two experts flew in from the United States and the art world on the other side of the Atlantic was electrified.

The most famous American painter in the middle years of the nineteenth century was Frederic Edwin Church, and the most striking of his works were three enormous canvases, always referred to as his 'Great Pictures'. One of them, painted in 1861, was a portrayal of an Arctic landscape. Its original title was *The Icebergs* but at the outbreak of the Civil War Church renamed it *The North* as a patriotic reference to the Northern Union in the War. Advertisements for the exhibition noted that the admission proceeds would be donated to the Patriotic Fund, which supported Union soldiers' families.

Because of the turbulence of the Civil War, when nobody wanted to risk spending money, and perhaps because of its size, the painting failed to find a buyer in the United States. Church decided in 1863 to ship it to London, the wealthiest city in the wealthiest country in the world. Since the British were at the time supporting the Southern States in the Civil War, Church judiciously changed the name of the painting back to its original non-political title, *The Icebergs*. It was exhibited at the German Gallery in New Bond Street and was a sensation. Church had painted in an extra detail, aimed specially at the British market. Some years before, Sir John Franklin, the great British explorer, had disappeared on an expedition to navigate the North West Passage in the Canadian Arctic, the only northern way by sea from the Atlantic to the Pacific Oceans and therefore of great potential value as a trading route. Franklin's tragic death along with his entire crew had turned him into a national hero in Britain. To capitalise on the public's interest, Church invited Franklin's widow to the exhibition in London and added a forlorn crow's nest and a broken mast to the foreground of his painting. The publicity worked and the painting was sold for £10,000. That would be the equivalent of half a million pounds today, though in an inflated art market the picture would fetch tens of millions of pounds.

The buyer was anonymous and *The Icebergs* disappeared from public view. It was to be more than a hundred years before it was seen again.

By the 1970s Church's paintings were in great demand in the United States and Canada and his large paintings were now regarded as masterpieces. Two were hanging in prestigious galleries in New York and Washington. Where was the third, *The Icebergs*?

In 1977 an American art historian, Sandra Feldman, set out to discover if *The Icebergs* still existed. She narrowed the possible buyers down to three. One was Edward Watkin of Rose Hill in Manchester, England. To her surprise she discovered that the house still existed. But when she researched further she found it wasn't a promising lead. Rose Hill Remand Home for delinquent boys was hardly likely to be a centre of culture. She phoned the home from New York but without success.

Sandra Feldman would not take no for an answer. She contacted the head of the local history library in Manchester to ask if he could get her an introduction into Rose Hill. Another disappointment. He could not have been more discouraging. She said later that he made the remand home sound like a high-security prison. There was no way that members of the public would be allowed to visit it. In any case he did not have the time or the inclination to accompany her.

Sandra Feldman had worked so hard to find the painting, but the trail had gone cold. She gave up, which was a pity since *The Icebergs* was in Rose Hill. The anonymous buyer had been Edward Watkin, though he had arranged for a friend to make the actual purchase as he himself was out of the country at the time of the auction.

What led Watkin to pay a considerable amount of money for a painting by an artist unknown in Britain at the time? One reason could have been prestige. A man of his wealth and standing in society would have been expected to display valuable paintings and statues in his mansion and he and his wife had created an art gallery at Rose Hill. But there may have been more personal reasons why he was attracted to *The Icebergs*. In the early 1860s he had published his book *Canada and the States: Recollections*. In it he showed how fascinated he had been by the power and beauty of the icebergs during his frequent journeys across the Atlantic:

> We had heard that icebergs had been seen and at 3 o'clock we saw ahead of us something which looked like the wreck of a steamer. It was about 10 miles off. We found it was a mountain of ice, covering perhaps a couple of acres in area, and about 50 or 60 feet high. It assumed all sorts of shapes as we caught sight of it at different points – it looked, once, like a great lion crouching on the water – then it took an appearance like part of the causeway at Staffa. As soon as we got abreast of it we saw pack ice around it, and the light, then shining upon the whole mass, gave a fairy-like whiteness – transparent, snowy whiteness – which was very beautiful to see. While we were observing it, a great mass broke away, toppled over into the sea, sending up an immense snowy spray, and disappeared.

What must have given icebergs extra meaning for Watkin was that the time when Frederic Church put his painting on sale in London coincided with the period when Watkin was secretly involved in the negotiations that led to the birth of a new country, the Dominion of Canada, with its vast areas of permanent snow and ice. The reports by local journalists referred to earlier show that Rose Hill was a treasure trove of Watkin's public life. What better symbol of his secret work on behalf of a member of the Cabinet than a painting from the Northern waters off the American continent?

Finally, the characters of Frederic Church and the Railway King were very similar. According to the writer John Updike, Church was 'a showman, Barnumesque, drawn to subjects with an element of spectacle – flaming sunsets, glaring icebergs, erupting volcanoes.' The parallels with the character of Edward Watkin, described by that earlier writer as motivated by the desire to do something 'stupendous', are irresistible. The love of dramatic spectacle that led Church to create his painting is echoed in Watkin's excitement at the sweep of grand projects.

Whatever the reasons for Watkin's purchase of the painting, the story of its rediscovery after more than a hundred years is fascinating. After Sandra Feldman retired defeated from her search another woman enters the story of *The Icebergs*, the matron at Rose Hill Remand Home, Mrs Mair Baulch. Much of what follows draws on her own account, given here for the first time.

It started with Mair's dream. She wanted to help the boys in her care to get jobs when they had finished their sentences at the remand home. She wanted to buy a dilapidated cottage in the Derbyshire Peak District for them to do up by putting their craft lessons to practical use and to see the countryside. Mair said that one of the boys had never seen a cow till they saw one in the fields at Rose Hill. On the landing outside her top-floor flat in Rose Hill was an old painting. Mair asked her boss, the director of Social Services in Manchester, for permission to try to sell it to raise money for her project. No problem, said the director – after all, nobody else had ever shown any interest in it. His precise words to her were: 'Go ahead if you want but you won't get £100 for it.'

Mair, an art lover, started to research the painting's origins. She began with the signature on it, F.E. Church, and the date, 1861. She discovered that the artist was an American. During a holiday in Chicago she had visited that city's Art Institute and remembered seeing a number of paintings in a similar style so she wrote to Chicago to ask if they would be interested in the painting at Rose Hill. They said they might be.

Mair was pleased how helpful the Americans seemed, particularly when they sent a telegram to say that the curator would like to fly to Manchester and bring one of the Institute's trustees along. The Americans took two days to examine the picture and took Mair and her husband out to the best local restaurant. But on their return home they wrote to Mair with discouraging news. The painting was probably a copy. Anyway, someone had put a 14in-wide border on it, the implication being that this had reduced its value, though it might be worth a few thousand pounds. However, they were willing to pay the cost of shipping the picture to Chicago for it to be examined further. They pointed out that this was a generous exception to their normal practice.

Something about the letter made Mair uneasy. Why had two such important people flown at very short notice from the United States, taken two days just to examine the painting and, although it was probably a copy, were willing, exceptionally, to pay to have it flown to the United States for further examination? There was also the way the letter seemed to go on a bit about the Institute's credentials. The curator emphasised to her that they would be 'extremely fair' in their dealings with her and wrote: 'You know our museum. The international status of it will assure your board that we would not, indeed could not, take any action which was anything but honourable.'

There is a saying by an American poet, Ralph Waldo Emerson: 'The louder he spoke of his honor, the faster we counted our spoons.'

Mair was right to be suspicious. She would have been even more suspicious if she had known that a book had been published in the United States about Church's landscape paintings, with an image of a chromolithograhic reproduction of *The Icebergs* on its dust jacket. The whole art world in America knew that the painting had disappeared after being sold in Britain and one of the visitors from Chicago was an art expert and the other a trustee of the Institute. There was no evidence that a full-sized copy of the painting had ever been made. Of course, Mair knew none of this. She also didn't know that the trustee who had examined the painting had said in an interview the year before that he came from a line of successful crooks. He later said that 'crooks' was the wrong word but added: 'My ancestors were ruthless businessmen, who did what it took to win.' Mair reported to her director what had happened. From now on, everything was taken out of her hands. It is clear from copies of correspondence at the time that the senior managers of the City Council shared her suspicions. They decided to send colour photographs of the painting and the signature on it to the famous art auctioneers Sotheby's, in London. The story moved up a gear. Sotheby's contacted their New York branch. When the staff there saw the photos, they 'shrieked with excitement'. Sotheby's told their London specialist, James Miller, to get to Rose Hill, and quickly. Imagine his feelings when he found the painting hanging on a landing just under the roof. He was looking at a masterpiece that had been missing for over a hundred years.

Sotheby's knew that word of the discovery of *The Icebergs* would soon leak out. They also knew that the painting would fetch far more in New

York than in London. Their New York specialist stayed up all night just to be awake for when Miller got into work next morning, London time. She flew to London the same day with a proposed contract for Sotheby's to have exclusive rights to the auction. The City Council was short of money at the time and in spite of protests by the head of the city's art gallery, who wanted to keep the painting in Manchester, they saw the painting as a 'windfall', to keep the rates down. The deal between Manchester and Sotheby's was soon done.

A group of teachers at Rose Hill was asked to help take the painting from its upstairs wall and bring it down Rose Hill's imposing staircase. That was easier said than done. The screws holding the painting were 12in long and had been in place nearly sixty years. They were impossible to move. Fortunately, one of the teachers had started work at Rose Hill as a craft teacher. He had a friend who was a local wood merchant and let him borrow the only 4ft screwdriver in Manchester. (Galileo said: 'Give me a lever long enough and I shall move the world.') The screws moved and the staff and a senior boy lifted *The Icebergs* down from the wall and started to carry it down the staircase, no mean task for a heavy canvas (5ft by 10ft), not including its ornate Victorian frame. All went well until they reached the bottom of the stairs, which ended at a wall at right angles. Those last feet called for a tricky manoeuvre, particularly as the staircase had, as with all stairs, an upright pole called a newel post that holds the structure of the staircase together. Sticking up on top of the newel post was a decorative wooden finial ball and the painting had to be lifted over that and at the same time turned in a confined space. The staff team had paused to plan out this last crucial move when one of the teachers saw to his horror that the young man who was helping was supporting the weight of the painting on his head. If the teacher had not shouted a warning the canvas would have had a hole punched in it, which would have reduced the value of the masterpiece somewhat.

Meanwhile, word of the proposed sale of *The Icebergs* had caused anger in Northenden. One of the elders of St Wilfrid's Church demanded that the painting should be handed back to the people of the parish, its owners in perpetuity as a result of Mr Parkyn's gift in 1915. Representatives of the church came to Rose Hill without notice 'to pick up their painting' but they were 2 hours late – it had been taken to the Town Hall, where it was stored in an air-conditioned warehouse until it could be flown to the United States.

The scene moved to New York, where the stage was set for the grand finale of this unique story. On the morning of 25 October 1979, *The Icebergs*, its magnificent colours now fully restored, was put up for auction at Sotheby's as Lot 34. The sale had attracted enormous interest in the United States and Canada, fuelled by the fashion for Church's paintings and press interest in the intriguing story of the re-discovery of *The Icebergs*. The normally staid *New York Times* described the painting as 'rosy, emerald, white and shimmering'.

The *Texas Journal* of April 1980 captured the drama of the sale in these words:

> The first 33 paintings went in brisk auction-house style. The auctioneer, Sotheby's president, John Marion, would ask for an opening bid at a pre-assigned minimum price, and bidders would signal – with nods, waves, shouts, or flicks of their pens – their willingness to go along with successive price increases. Each sale took only seconds, but tension built as each lot was picked off, and when Marion announced, 'Lot 34', the spectators buzzed loudly and then grew silent. Marion asked for the opening bid – $500,000. In increments of $50,000, the price went up rapidly, propelled by about eight or ten bidders. Two of them were bidding via telephone linkups with Sotheby's personnel in the auditorium. Within thirty seconds *The Icebergs* had gone beyond the $1 million mark. At 1.5 million, the museums and galleries dropped out of the competition; only private collectors could justify maintaining the bidding beyond that point. The climb towards 2 million began, punctuated by increasingly long pauses as the handful of remaining buyers hesitated, then rushed ahead. Each time the chase was taken up again, the crowd oohed and aahed appreciatively. There was a gasp when the 2 million barrier was reached. At that point only two telephone bidders were left, to go head to head Marion broke the sequence of 50,000 price hikes and asked for $100 thousand increments from now on. The unidentified callers remained locked in combat, as the bidding leapfrogged skyward. 'And two million, five hundred thousand?' Marion queried into the microphone. A pause followed. He got it. And then, somewhere out there a very wealthy individual decided to let go of a prize for which he was willing to pay $2.4 million but not $2.6million. It was over. The crowd cheered and broke into applause.

$2.5 million. Two-and-a-half times what anyone had ever paid for any painting in the United States at auction. $2.5 million at today's prices is £4 million.

The *New York Times* reported:

Immediately after the auction had ended, James P. Miller, Sotheby specialist in paintings who lives in London and who originally recognized the painting as a Church from a photograph, placed a trans-Atlantic call to the sellers of the work in Manchester to relay the news of the record price. He spoke with C.A. Hilditch, director of Manchester Social Services, owners of Rose Hill, a reformatory for boys that had decided to dispose of the painting to raise funds for maintaining and improving the institution. 'There was a prolonged silence,' Mr. Miller reported. 'After all, the painting went for more than double their wildest hopes.' Then, Mr. Miller said, Mr. Hilditch spoke: 'It's a very good bit of news at the end of a hard day.'

The sale of *The Icebergs* in New York did not see the end of the affair. Many people in the parish of Northenden maintained that the painting had been a gift to them in perpetuity. For a year the lawyers of the Council and the Charities Commission wrangled and the matter went to the High Court in London. The Council claimed that as they were the owners of Rose Hill and had been the legal representatives of the people of Northenden since 1931, when Cheshire Northenden had been incorporated into the city, the painting belonged to Manchester. The Council won and used the money to keep down the rates.

Rose Hill's bank account with the Council, which already contained the million pounds from the sale of the Watkin lands and the house, was now well in the black but Mrs Baulch never got the cottage for her lads. Contrary to the report in the *New York Times*, the profit from *The Icebergs* went into Manchester's general funds.

The Icebergs' journey had started from New York in 1863. From London it had gone to Rose Hill, to be loved by the Railway King for the rest of his life, then dumped at the back of the Church Rooms in Northenden village and sent back to Rose Hill when it got in the way of some amateur actors. It had remained at Rose Hill, growing grubbier, for fifty-eight more years, in full view but in reality unseen because nobody was interested enough to look at it.

In June 1979 it was hanging on a wall in a remand home, worth next to nothing. Four months later it had returned to New York in triumph after an absence of 116 years and been sold for a fortune.

The buyers remained anonymous but they donated it to what is now the Dallas Museum of Art, where it is on permanent display. The Museum describes it as the 'Mona Lisa' of their collection.

There are two footnotes to the story of *The Icebergs*.

To avoid publicity, the painting was packed in an ordinary crate for its journey to Texas and labelled 'Household Items'. The airline was not let in on the secret and since they were dealing with what was apparently just an everyday item of freight they did not give it priority. As there was no room for it on the first flight to Dallas it was left out on the tarmac of the airport overnight and only put on a plane 24 hours later.

The last word on the remarkable story of the discovery of the lost masterpiece must rest with Edith Belson, the author's aunt. She worked at Rose Hill Remand Home in the late 1950s as a secretary. She remembered the painting. One day she said to her boss: 'That's a nice painting.' He said: 'Do you want it?' She said: 'Where would I find room for a painting that size in a council house?' Soon afterwards she left Rose Hill. The rest, as they say, is history.

The story of Rose Hill, the house that rose and fell and rose again, has – along with the stories of Absalom and Edward Watkin – been forgotten, even in Northenden and the city of Manchester. Yet, in spite of its near-death, it remains one of only a small number of historic buildings in England that have been awarded that star status in the national listing. Great plans such as the repeal of the Corn Laws were hatched within its walls and a succession of the most famous figures of the 1800s stepped across its threshold. It is now in private hands with apartments in the place of the Watkins' library, art gallery, dining room, ballroom and walled garden. But its history remains and the outside of what that advertisement for the new housing estate in 1994 called 'the Great House' still looks as it did in Edward's day. Something to treasure, not only as part of the Edward Watkin story but also – thanks to its listed building status – as part of Britain's heritage.

Chapter 15

Time to Remember Edward Watkin

In light of all his activities it is remarkable that today Edward Watkin has been almost totally forgotten. This was the man who had been described in that magazine article in 1879 as the acknowledged chief of the railway system of the United Kingdom and therefore of the world. Another article in a prestigious volume in 1893 with the title *Our Celebrities – A Portrait Gallery* compiled by Valery, 'Photographer to the Queen', reviews his achievements:

> At the desire of the then Secretary of State for the Colonies, the Duke of Newcastle, Sir EDWARD went to Canada in 1861, and virtually brought about the union of the five British provinces, and the establishment of the great Canadian railway system. Perhaps Sir EDWARD is the only man in the world who has purchased and paid for a continent. His acquisition, in 1863, of the Hudson's Bay property for £1,500,000 was remarkable.

At his death eight years after that article appeared his reputation seemed assured. The hundreds of newspapers in Britain and throughout the world that recorded his passing, including the *New York Times* and the *Sydney Morning Herald*, were proof of his stature. An obituary in *The London Times* that referred to his 'qualities of greatness' was typical of the judgments of his contemporaries. The *Manchester Guardian*'s obituary said: 'The name he left behind is one of which his fellow citizens have every reason to be proud'.

Yet only a week after his death an event occurred which in a small way anticipated the long period of decline in reputation which was about to follow. The funeral took place at St Wilfrid's and special trains were laid on from Central Station in Manchester to Northenden. The mourners included representatives of all Britain's railway companies and the Mayor of Folkestone (the town he had represented in Parliament) and several of its councillors. Also present was the most eminent geologist of the day, Professor Sir Richard Boyd Dawkins, who twenty years before had provided expert support for Watkin on the feasibility of a Channel tunnel. (He wrote later to a friend: 'I always found Sir Edward a generous and straightforward imperious friend. He did not care for money and died a poor man, when he might have accumulated great wealth. His railways were in bad care when he acted as railway doctor.') Yet, apart from family, friends and official representatives and the villagers of Northenden, only a hundred people were present at the funeral. The contrast with his wife's funeral thirteen years earlier is striking. Many of those famous people expressing sympathy in 1888 would not have known Mary but Watkin's star was still shining back then. Now they were absent. Only three MPs attended Edward's funeral in 1901 and two of those were present in their official capacity as officers of one of Watkin's railway companies. The list of official mourners contains one particularly glaring omission: nobody from Manchester City Council attended. The day when he and his fellow fundraiser for Manchester and Salford's first Parks for the People had been greeted with prolonged applause at a special meeting of the City Council in Manchester Town Hall was long forgotten. Perhaps Watkin, never a team player, had given the city the impression that although he continued to live only a few miles away in Northenden he had outgrown Manchester. He had – and this must have been resented. Men like Brunel, who is recorded as having spoken in Parliament 233 times in support of railway bills, and Watkin, with 173 such entries, belonged, as one commentator wrote: 'to a new international world of big business and negotiated as equals with prime ministers and emperors'. Not local councillors.

Manchester's snub at Watkin's funeral in 1901 looks petty from this distance. Yet over a century since his death the only commemoration in the city that mentions his name is a recently erected plaque in one of the parks he made possible. For sixty-five years his home was in what is now a Manchester suburb. He died there and he is buried in a Manchester churchyard. The city's neglect of his achievements, local, national and international, lacks the perspective of history.

Watkin's reputation beyond Manchester has not weathered well either. He soon became Yesterday's Man. Not until 2002 and 2005, when David Hodgkins and John Greaves published their pioneering and scholarly accounts of his railway work, was a hundred years of obscurity broken. His achievements have otherwise been largely overlooked and any references to him highlight only his failures, his tetchy battles with other railway chairmen and the low dividends of the companies he controlled, ignoring the fact that – as Professor Dawkins pointed out – the Railway Doctor was always called in to take over companies that were close to bankruptcy. Many judgments of him are negative, with the most extreme being Simmons, the railway historian, who called him a megalomaniac. Today, only the frequency with which Watkin's name pops up in books and TV programmes hints at the range of his activities. But even then it is only ever as a footnote. Yet we are dealing here with a man who played a key role in the birth of the second biggest country in the world, created the world's largest fishing port, built the last main line into London for a hundred years and took on the political and military establishment of Britain with his astonishing and visionary plan to tunnel under the English Channel.

Some footnote.

Why did Watkin's reputation decline so dramatically? There are three explanations.

First, his two great failures, the Channel tunnel, and the Wembley Tower, were so spectacular that even in his lifetime they overshadowed his triumphs. He hit the newspaper headlines after he took the government to the High Court when they stopped him digging his tunnel – and he lost. His refusal to admit defeat meant that he returned to the issue time and time again in the Commons. The mocking of the 'Bore of the Channel Tunnel' increased with each defeat: 'Here he goes again.' Then the breathtaking Wembley Tower became the rusting hulk of 'Watkin's Folly', a looming and constant monument to his failure on the North London horizon until it was dismantled and sold as scrap metal. Even his tremendous enterprise, the Great Central Railway, which he achieved virtually single-handed in the face of enormous and bitter opposition, was never seen as a success. It was the only main-line railway to be axed by Dr Beeching in his myopic 1963 report, though fifty years later it enjoyed a brief flirtation with the Labour Party, when they wondered whether what remains of the line could be put up as a cheaper alternative to High Speed 2. Otherwise, it has been forgotten, except by railway buffs.

The second reason why Watkin has been forgotten stems from his restless need to be moving on to new schemes. Some of the enterprises which he lent his name to appear at a century's distance to have been trivial and adopted just for effect. Others, although they were on a dramatic and exciting scale, called into question his judgement. Transatlantic boat crossings from America to Britain ended in those days with a detour round the island of Ireland. He planned to take days off the journey by cutting Ireland in half. He would dig a 110-mile-long canal from Dublin Bay to Galway Bay, the same length as the recently opened Suez Canal. It was a strange venture since it ignored the obvious problem that since ocean-going liners would have to drop their speed dramatically while passing through the canal there would not have been enough saving of time to justify the enormous cost. It was an unrealistic pipedream. His failure to require a proper survey of the ground under the colossal weight of his Eiffel Tower at Wembley was disastrous. When, short of money, he reduced the number of its legs, thus increasing the pressure on each, the tower began to tilt.

The result of the extraordinary scope and the drama of his projects meant that Watkin attempted too much and spread the butter of his energy too thinly. The jack of all trades and master of none label stuck. The range of his interests was incredible, but his life lacked a single peg to hang fame on to. This lack of focus had its effect on his parliamentary career. After showing such high and early potential and having as his supporter one of the most powerful parliamentarians in Richard Cobden, he failed to make an impact in Parliament and never rose higher than backbencher and chairman of two financial sub-committees.

Apart from his behind-the-scenes activities in Canada, carrying out satisfyingly top-secret work on behalf of the British government, Watkin was never a team player. If politics is the art of the possible, success in party politics is the art of making allies and that was Watkin's weakness. One result of his independence was that he never developed a power base in the House of Commons. When he needed friends, particularly during his eleven attempts to get a Channel tunnel bill through, there was little rallying of support for him. In fact, many MPs who had suffered his barbs must have seen the failure of the tunnel as payback time. In all his years in the Commons Watkin made only one major ally, Gladstone, and he even parted company with him over Home Rule for Ireland. Where ambitious MPs take the long view and are prepared to defer to senior members of a party Watkin let it be known that he was right and that those who disagreed with him were wrong. The speed of Nimble Ned's mind meant that he must have often been impatient with lesser mortals when progress was slow – and showed it. His unwillingness to compromise also meant that he could not be relied on to toe a party line. He prided himself on his ability to 'think outside the box'. His pragmatism first showed itself in that invitation to Disraeli in order to boost the numbers for the soirées at the Free Trade Hall in Manchester, at a time when Disraeli was an arch opponent of everything Edward and his father had fought for during the Corn Law campaign. Such considerations took second place to Edward's immediate aim, which was to sell tickets and wipe out the Manchester Athenaeum's debt.

A seat in the House of Commons was useful in providing contacts and keeping up with the latest developments but the demands made on him by his many other interests entailed such frequent and prolonged absences from Parliament and indeed the country that his fellow MPs and particularly the party leaders must have soon realised that he was a part-time MP. Even by the time he had secured his seat at Stockport in 1864, the focus of his energies had moved elsewhere. He was in the middle of his activities in Canada and making frequent journeys across the Atlantic, even the fastest of which took three weeks for the round trip. As the feisty chairman of the expanding MSLR he had the big prize, a main line into London, in his sights and he needed time to work on it. When Cobden wrote his letter of support before the Yarmouth campaign in 1857, Watkin was a relatively young man. His energy, experience and charisma marked him out as having high political potential. A glittering political career beckoned (as it had done for his father). Instead, he chose to dominate the railways, the dominant industry of the world's dominant country. Jam today and all those opportunities to prove himself, without having to wait on party patronage.

The third reason why Watkin has been so undervalued since his death is that assessments of his importance have always been too narrow: restricted to the railways and to Britain. Of course, his railway achievements were immense, as reflected in the titles of the two biographies: *The Last of the Railway Kings* and *The Second Railway King*. In view of the colossal time he spent as chairman or director of so many railway companies and his mastery of the key Victorian industry, 'railway entrepreneur' would seem to be a fair summary of his life. But it isn't. This closer examination of his life has shown that the railways were not the whole man. His most significant success was in Canada, not Britain, and went far beyond the rescue of a railway line.

What interested Watkin in Canada stemmed from something which – in the mass of details in his many schemes – has been largely ignored but which was actually central to the man. In the middle of all his ripping wheezes and top-doggery he had a sense of vision. He was, as one writer said, 'a great and picturesque figure, far above the ordinary man'. When the list of ideas, large and small, that captured his attention, even if only temporarily, is set out in full, the extent of his ability to challenge established thinking and see beyond the immediate horizon is revealed: the potential for growth in Canada, Grimsby and Metroland; replacing the piecemeal railway system in Britain (still evident today) with a coherent system as in all other major countries; his leisure park in rural Wembley, miles away from where the customers lived; his highlighting of the dead-end termini of major cities which even today prevent through-running; the concern for the well-being of Ireland that he shared with his father. Watkin was a big man, with ideas that were often too big for his powers. He had a sense of a larger world than Little England, which even at the height of Britain's power in the second half of the nineteenth century showed that genius for practical short-termism, tactics rather than strategy, which can also be a weakness, as Goethe pointed out.

It was in his vision of a railway underneath the English Channel that Watkin came closest to achieving greatness. He knew that his tunnel was a practical proposition. Professor Dawkins had surveyed it and found that the continuous layer of sedimentary chalk between Dover and Calais was ideal material for tunnelling, stable, non-porous and easy to work. What the engineers digging the present Channel Tunnel at the end of the twentieth century found when they broke through into Watkin's tunnel proved that France and Britain could have been linked more than a hundred years earlier. But it was not the mechanics of construction that defeated him. What destroyed his grand plan was the timid politics of the Establishment and the press of the time. It is the final irony that Watkin the politician was in the end defeated by politics.

The completion of a tunnel under the English Channel in the last decade of the nineteenth century would have transformed the economic and social history of Western Europe. Over the years easier traffic would have nibbled away at the resistance to closer ties with the Continent that still dominates the politics of Britain (or rather of England). The consequences for what was in Watkin's time still a single country, including

Ireland, would have been profound. Watkin had wanted to link Ireland to Britain by a rail tunnel near Stranraer. That tunnel, with a main line running through his Channel tunnel to link up with the European rail network, would have brought a poor and rural country into the economic mainstream of Europe and transformed the Irish economy and its history, a cause that stirred both Edward and his father.

By the time of Watkin's death in 1901 the old certainties about British power and insular mindsets had begun to wobble. From 10 to 17 December 1899, what was called at the time Black Week, the great British Army suffered three devastating defeats at the hands of the Boers in South Africa. These signalled the end of the rule of the complacent old guard, which Wolseley had represented, and the army's position began to change in line with the national mood. Relations between the old enemies, France and Britain, had been improving for some years. Bismarck, the great nineteenth-century German Chancellor, said that nothing unites people so much as a common enemy and the rising power and aggression of Germany drove France and Britain together. Queen Victoria's successor, Edward VII, charmed the French on a state visit in 1901 and in 1904 the Entente Cordiale was signed between Britain and France as a symbol of their new friendship.

The most intriguing of the many 'What Ifs' in Watkin's life is what if he had been born twenty years later and survived till the 1920s. With his fascination for innovation he would have relished the dawn of the car and plane eras. He would have seen the back of his old adversaries, Lord Wolseley and Joseph Chamberlain, who died in 1913 and 1914. Best of all, his Channel tunnel, a product of the new Anglo-French accord, would have been ready for the movement of heavy armaments to the Continent that one field marshal said in 1922 would have repulsed the German advance into France in 1914 and shortened the First World War by two years. Prime Minister David Lloyd George would have added Watkin's tunnel to the praise he did give for the Great Central Railway's key role in transporting soldiers and weapons inside Britain. The peerage that he longed for would have been his as a grateful nation finally soothed his itch for recognition.

In 1914 Great Britain took a major step that significantly altered its status as an island, divorced from its geographical neighbours. It entered what for the next three years, until the United States joined in, was known as the Great European War. By 1918 nearly 1 million dead from Britain and its Empire showed that the 22-mile-wide English Channel, the silver streak which God had provided as protection, was after all only water – to be crossed or tunnelled, not to be hidden behind.

An article in the *Observer* newspaper on 16 March 1919 reflected the change in Britain's view of itself, though its confident optimism about the tunnel was, to say the least, premature. 'The war has changed all things. Our insularity has gone. England is no longer an island. It is a Continental Power. We have a new perspective. The Tunnel has become a necessity.' The article singled out Sir Edward Watkin as 'one of the pioneers who, in face of much opposition, and at great sacrifices, kept on with their dream'.

Another sign of the new Anglo-French relationship was the appointment in 1918 of the French Field Marshal Ferdinand Foch as Commander-in-Chief of all the Allied armies. A few days after the war ended, King George V admitted him to the Order of Merit, an award in the personal gift of the sovereign and once described as 'possibly the most prestigious honour one can receive on Planet Earth'. It was Foch who said that a Channel tunnel would have shortened the First World War by two years.

Just how visionary Watkin was in seeing the potential for long-distance rail traffic is only now becoming clear. He would have been laughed at if he had let it be generally known that his ultimate goal was to build a railway line not just to Paris but to Baghdad and India. Yet forty trains a month are now transporting freight between China and Germany, Spain, nine states of the former Soviet Union and most recently a rail terminal in East London. The 8,000-mile journey by train takes twenty-one days. The equivalent journey by sea would take six weeks. As an ecological bonus, transport by road would cause three times as much carbon monoxide pollution.

One journalist called Edward Watkin 'The Nearly Man of Northenden'. There is just enough truth in that for it to be not just a snappy newspaper headline but only if an assessment of his life focuses on what he failed to achieve and ignores his successes. And even in his failures one of his most valuable characteristics can still be seen: an eagerness to take action. A German proverb, '*Aller Anfang ist schwer*', literally 'All beginning is difficult' contains what Jane Austen might have called a truth universally acknowledged: it is hard to overcome inertia. But not for Watkin. He had the knack of tackling what others thought impossible. His championing of a Channel tunnel at least kept the concept in the public eye after he and his geological expert, Professor Dawkins, showed that it could be done. He even chose the site of the twentieth-century tunnel. Similarly, he showed that an enormous public leisure park miles from the centre of London was feasible and ensured that the site had not been already covered in piecemeal houses and factories by the time it was needed for the Wembley Exhibition. He also provided the means for thousands to travel to it long after he was dead. His Grand Trunk Railway was the first building block for the Canadian Pacific Railway at a time when the Canadian railway system was in its infancy. Like John the Baptist, he was often a voice crying in the wilderness.

If he had succeeded in his daring vision of a tunnel under the English Channel the prize would have been the transformation of the economic structure and politics of Europe and history would have judged him to be one of the giants of his time. His lifelong itch to be famous would have been finally and satisfyingly scratched. But he staked his reputation on a single throw and he failed. When a timid British government barred the way to France in 1882, his place at the top table of history vanished.

There is one perhaps less important but nonetheless attractive reason for remembering Edward Watkin: the sense of excitement that he generated. This is captured in an interview he gave to a journalist from New Zealand which was published in January 1893. Because it is describing his current schemes it has an energy and freshness about it which articles looking back on history lack. In describing his great tower for example, he is talking about an exciting prospect, not a failure. At the age of 74 he is still making plans, the 'ingenious baronet', full of the enthusiasm that carried people along with his great schemes, even if – as the article shows – the details are not always thought through. Failure is not an option.

SIR EDWARD WATKIN AND HIS BIG SCHEMES

Although Sir Edward Watkin made his appointment to receive me at 9 o'clock in the morning, I found he had already commenced his busy day when I arrived. I was not kept waiting long in his comfortable suite of rooms in the Charing Cross Hotel before he entered.

The ingenious baronet is a short, thick-set gentleman, with greyish hair. He is extraordinarily young-looking for his age and might be in his prime judging from the energy and activity displayed in every movement. A stranger seeing him for the first time would put him down as not much over 40 years old, instead of nearly 80.

In conversation his countenance is continually animated. It is clear at once that he has that gift which goes so far to bring success – viz, enthusiasm in whatever he undertakes.

HIS ENGLISH EIFFEL TOWER

'You want to hear all about my various schemes. Well, then, starting with that which is most likely to be the first to arrive at a state of completion, the Great Tower for London, I will tell you as briefly as I can the facts that were announced a few days since at a meeting of shareholders in the enterprise. My idea is to set up at Wembley Park, which has been purchased and laid out for that purpose, a tower some 150ft higher than the Eiffel Tower in Paris. It is to be a pleasure resort of an almost unique character, as well as being a national curiosity and monument of engineering skill. It will be one of the greatest attractions for sightseers in the metropolis, and should draw thousands together. When they get to it, which they will do by a special station to be opened shortly by the Metropolitan Railway, they will find extensive grounds planned by the best landscape-gardeners of the day. In the centre will stand the gigantic structure, surrounded by stalls and booths of all kinds. A special feature will be very high-class dining and refreshment rooms. On entering the tower itself the visitor will discover that the lift accommodation is sufficient for 15,000 people to be on the tower at the same time. This is the lowest figure; probably it will be nearer 20,000 as a matter of fact. The lifts will take passengers up to the first platform, which will weigh 250 tons, and is to be covered over. There will be a large saloon or reception room for entertainments and dancing. Besides this there are to be 200 shops, with store cellars underneath them, whilst we shall provide any number of refreshment rooms and bars. Higher up again there is to be another landing stage surrounded by private dining rooms for dinner parties.

This is just a rough sketch of the idea, for it is not yet definitely settled. We expect that Mr Heenan, the builder of the Blackpool Tower, will undertake the contract, and we look forward to seeing the whole thing complete in about 18 months, at a cost of about £300,000, of which we have already spent £70,000 on the park. Besides being a pleasure resort, it should prove an inestimable blessing to the scientific world, and I anticipate an almost unequalled success for the undertaking, in proof of which I have backed my opinion by becoming the largest shareholder in the concern.

CUT IRELAND IN HALF

Ah, yes, the Irish canal scheme is another of my ideas. Here are the plans and the sections for it.'

And Sir Edward produced two large portfolios full of plans of every detail for the construction of an enormous ship canal to cut right across the centre of Ireland from Kingstown Harbour on the east to Galway Bay on the west.

'Of course, any quantity of money could be spent on the scheme, but it should be easily possible to complete it in accordance with these plans for an outlay of £8,000,000 sterling. The good derived from such a canal would soon repay this expenditure.

The benefits which it would confer both on Ireland itself, and upon the nation at large, can scarcely be over-estimated. In the first place, look at the untold advantage to be gained by all interested in transatlantic commerce by shortening the route to America by a clear day. Then, again, it would open up a direct road of communication into the very heart of Ireland. It would soon become one of the greatest trade highways in the world, and think what it would mean to a country to have such a highway passing through its centre.

But I have not yet been able to persuade the people of Great Britain that it is for their own good. And so we, for want of pluck, are likely to lose a source of wealth which lies at our very feet if we would but stretch out our hand and pick it up.

If our American and colonial cousins can bring off their mighty undertakings, why should we moulder from lack of energy to execute much smaller ones? What is an Irish canal compared to the trans-American railways, I should like to know.

Of course, it should be carried out by Government, and not by a private company, as it would be an Imperial benefit. As a matter of fact, I should like to see all railways in the hands of the Government.

By means of this canal Irish agricultural produce could be conveyed very cheaply to England or Scotland, and Ireland would, I believe, become the chief country in the world for dairy and farm produce.

Another of my schemes is, as you doubtless are aware, to make a tunnel between Ireland and Scotland where the sea is narrowest. This would cost, speaking quite roughly, about £10,000,000, and should be perfectly feasible. Works such as the St. Gothard Tunnel, the Severn Tunnel, the Mont Cenis Tunnel, all show what can be done in this direction.

No, I have quite given up the idea of a bridge from Scotland to Ireland, via the Isle of Man. It has been shown to be absolutely impracticable from technical considerations.

But there, friend, I must ask you to excuse me. Good-bye, and good luck to your enterprising journal.'

The excitement that Watkin could generate is visible in that contemporary account, so full of optimism. It is a feature of the man which detailed descriptions of his many failures and successes do not always reveal. In fact, the very weight of detail can obscure the air of adventure and risk that he had about him. It is only when you strip away the clutter and look at his life as a series of bullet points that you get a sense of the terrific impact he must have had in his lifetime. He was a showman who added to the gaiety of the nation, a ball rolling down a pin table, banging from one scheme to another, lights flashing and always making a noise.

Take a deep breath, put a coin in the slot and watch the ball roll: What he achieved:

- When he was in his early twenties he collected the money to buy the land for the first parks for the people of Salford and Manchester.
- he persuaded Manchester's business community to close on Saturday afternoons, seven years before the rest of Britain caught up
- he was a local councillor, an MP, a knight and a baronet
- he founded and wrote for a newspaper
- he wrote six books
- he developed Calais and Boulogne harbours to reduce their dependence on the tides in the Channel
- he turned Grimsby into the greatest fishing port in the world and its neighbour, Cleethorpes, into one of Britain's most popular holiday resorts

- he advised on railway systems in Europe, North America, Africa and India
- he transformed the bankrupt Grand Trunk Railway in Canada into the longest railway in the world
- he supported the move in Parliament to give votes to women, sixty-one years before Parliament changed the law
- he played a major role in the creation of the Dominion of Canada
- in his Manchester offices he installed electric lighting and pioneered the introduction of shorthand
- he enabled the Metropolitan Railway to profit from the most successful housing development in London's history
- he established a credit union bank for his employees
- he discovered coal under the sea off the coast of Kent and financed a new coalfield there
- he created a new footpath up Snowdon in Wales, the first in Britain dedicated solely for public use
- he created the Great Central Railway, the last main line into London till High Speed 1 in 2007

His unrealised pipe dreams included proposals to:

- dig a canal across Ireland to shorten the voyage from America to Britain
- link Hull to the wealthy south of England by a tunnel under the Humber
- turn Dungeness in Kent into a holiday resort
- link Ireland to Scotland by tunnel
- build two-storey carriages in order to double the capacity of trains and station platforms
- rebuild the terminus stations in the major UK cities so that trains could run through to further destinations
- build a railway from Manchester to India
- build a tower in London that would have out-eiffeled Eiffel
- dig a tunnel under the English Channel which would have transformed the history and economic structure of Europe

It is an amazing list. But although setting out those twenty-six bullet points is the best way to convey the sheer excitement of the Watkin story it does at the same time carry the risk of making him out to be a kind of dragonfly, brilliantly coloured but only skittering over the surface, a jack of all trades but master of none. Nothing could be further from the truth. This study of Watkin's life – his tunnel, his political work in Canada, his creation of a 186-mile-long railway into London, his imaginative scheme for an enormous leisure park miles from anywhere – all these have shown how profound and visionary his thinking could be, just two of the qualities of greatness referred to in that obituary in *The Times*.

Reminders in Britain today that Edward Watkin ever existed are few. There is a family memorial in St Wilfrid's Church, a few yards away from his grave and a mile away from what remains of Rose Hill. A diesel engine has been named *Sir Edward Watkin*. A few small streets named after him, including one at the back of Wembley Stadium. A plaque in one of the Manchester parks he created and another in Marylebone Station.

Curiously, one other reminder is at the side of one of the paths up Mount Snowdon, opened on 13 September 1892 by the then prime minister, William Ewart Gladstone. The idea for the path was conceived by Watkin after he read a newspaper article which advertised the sale of the south side of Snowdon in these words: 'Consider the enjoyment you will be able to give to thousands, the fishing, the climbing, and the joy of allowing people the freedom to ramble. There are few opportunities ever afforded a man to possess a park like this and know that people are all able to enjoy it without paying a farthing for it.' He bought the land, built himself a holiday chalet on part of it and on another section constructed a footpath up the mountain. As we saw with the fourth side of the plaque on the statue to Queen Victoria's husband in Grimsby, he was quite prepared to give himself credit if nobody else would so when Gladstone's opening speech failed to give him the credit for the scheme he erected a brass plate next to the path describing the occasion and ending with: 'THIS TABLET WAS PUBLICLY DEDICATED BY SIR EDWARD AND LADY WATKIN'.

One writer described the Watkin Path as the start of the Snowdonia National Park, opened sixty years later in 1951. It was the first path in Britain to be built and dedicated solely for the use of the public. One last first for Sir Edward. It is one of the most demanding routes up the mountain and in all the guidebooks it is still called the Watkin Path. (Its lesser fame is that it was used for the 1968 filming of *Carry on Up the Khyber*.) Close to it is a small example of Watkin's love of new ideas. His chalet was heated and lit by a small hydro-electric system. Fast-forward to 2011. Although the chalet was no more by then, the turbines that Watkin created were unearthed. Now, several features of his original system, including its small lake and original pipe work, are being used as part of a twenty-first-century technology project.

Behind the sheer breadth of Watkin's ideas, his successes and his failures, lay a complex and fascinating character, not easily bottled and sold. One writer, trying to sum the man up, showed the complexity by listing a jumble of qualities in one sentence: 'quixotic, hyperactive, arrogant, dictatorial, acerbic, self-made, status-conscious'. All true but he omitted to add: 'witty, charming, generous, forgiving, loyal'.

The existing literature about Edward Watkin, including the many footnotes to articles that refer to him briefly, concentrates on his railway activity. In that field he had many opponents and Disraeli spoke for them in describing him as wary, watchful and aggressive. His compulsive need to win every battle must have often led him to go over the top and show poor judgment. As a result, most writers have made the mistake of portraying Watkin's aggressiveness as being the whole man. But the Edward Watkin revealed in his diaries and many contemporary accounts is not like that. There are many references to his generous nature. He did not bear grudges. His friendly correspondence with, for example, his arch-enemy in the Channel tunnel battle, Lord Wolseley, is just one example. This generosity showed through in the way he identified and promoted potential in 'Watkin's young men'. Most dominant men cannot tolerate rivals. Another side to his generosity must explain why this multi-millionaire left only just over £17,000, a relatively small amount commented on by his friend, Professor Dawkins.

There are many contemporary references to his cheerfulness when he was defeated and the total absence of scandal in a life full of business battles and vengeful enemies cannot be explained away only by his eagerness to turn to the courts to protect his reputation. He is often appealingly vulnerable, as shown in his letter to the first Prime Minister of Canada when he had been snubbed, and his undignified, rather sad attempts to solicit a baronetcy in later life.

One of the obituaries in his daughter's album now in the Chetham's Library captures the attractive side of Watkin's character:

In private life he was the very antitype of himself as a public man; a cultivated, pleasant and often entertaining companion, a most genial host, and frequently a good friend. There are many among us still who owe much to his friendship and generosity, and it is not of every man in the position occupied by Sir Edward Watkin that this much can be truly said. It is pleasant to be able to temper one's criticisms of an old adversary who is now no more by an admission of virtues which after all atone for many faults.

As the last sentence hints, the publication in which this tribute appeared, the *Railway Times,* had often been highly critical of Watkin's railway career. That makes the generosity of its final words all the more powerful. They are matched by the affectionate but forward-looking obituary published by one of the newspapers in the city which never honoured his death, the *Manchester Evening News:*

It was inevitable in an ambitious career that some of his pet schemes should not be wholly successful, though he probably never admitted to himself that they had really and finally failed. We may be pretty sure that he died under the impression deep down in his heart of hearts that the Chanel Tunnel, which ordinary and unimaginative critics may regard as one of his failures, will some day become the magnificent reality he pictured, that abundant coal will reveal itself to Kent, and that if any of his favourite plans and undertakings seem to hang fire time will right them. It is pleasant to think that the close of Sir Edward's really wonderful career has been peaceful and so far as is possible for such a nature, reposeful. In the calm beauty of the Welsh Alps he found a home after his own desires and in the quietude of the still pretty Manchester suburb, quiet yet still within the sound of the boom of the Big Ben of Manchester Town Hall, he fought his last fight.

Christopher Wren, Britain's greatest architect, lived in an age which erected statues to everyone in public life. Yet there is no statue to Wren in London, the city graced by his loveliest buildings. If you go to his finest London church, St Paul's Cathedral, and stand under its great dome you will see a Latin inscription etched in a circle in the marble floor: '*Si monumentum requires, circumspice*' – 'If you seeking his monument, just look all around you'.

A knowledgeable traveller on one of the great railway journeys of the world through the Canadian Rockies or on Eurostar going through the Channel Tunnel or on what remains of the Great Central Railway in Middle England or visiting friends in Metroland or having a walk in one of Manchester's parks or looking at *The Icebergs* hanging in pride of place in the Dallas Museum of Art or getting off at Wembley Park Station or going to watch a match on a pitch built over the lost Great Tower in London or walking up Snowdon on the Watkin Path, could echo that tribute to Christopher Wren.

Any one of those destinations would be good reason for remembering the most worthy Sir Edward William Watkin, Baronet, JP, MP, High Sheriff of Cheshire, Officer of the Order of Leopold of Belgium, Officer of the Order of the Redeemer of Greece, director or chairman of a host of railway companies but also a visionary and a dreamer of dreams and at the same time a fizzer called Nimble Ned, who was always giving that extra ninepence in order to get to the top of the tree – and nearly made it.

Epilogue

It seems that, after all, the often sad story of Edward Watkin might have a happy ending. The years of oblivion for Rose Hill House and its once famous occupant are passing. This book and numerous requests for presentations about Edward Watkin are two straws in the wind. In 2015 a group of Northenden residents formed themselves into the Friends of Rose Hill, with the twin aims of publicising the history of the Watkin family and protecting Absalom's woods in front of the family home from decline. In their campaign for the Rose Hill Woods they had the support of the City Council, the owners of the woods, and 'A Life for a Life', an Oldham-based charity whose main aim is to plant and care for trees in memory of family members and treasured events but also to encourage community initiatives. In 2016 the Friends worked for a year with a small group of young people as part of a project researching Watkin's life. This was financed by an award from the National Heritage Lottery Fund.

Encouraged by the success of the young people's scheme the Friends drew up an ambitious plan to publicise the Watkin story and applied for a further award from the National Heritage Lottery Fund. In January 2018 this was granted. Links were set up with the headteachers and staff of two local primary schools, who incorporated Absalom and Edward in their National Curriculum work with 120 children, including drama, art and creative writing on the Watkin theme. A banner depicting the Watkin story was created by the children of one of the schools and is now on permanent display in St Wilfrid's Church. With the permission of St Wilfrid's Parochial Council and family descendants the Watkin graves were cleaned and their lettering restored. A line was added to Absalom's gravestone to commemorate his mother, who is buried in that derelict churchyard in north Manchester. A booklet about Nimble Ned and a short film were published along with illustrated leaflets setting out the history of the Watkins and a Watkin Walk for residents and visitors, beginning at the church and ending at Rose Hill Woods and the house.

Another part of the lottery grant was used to revive the woods, which are open to the public. Two of Absalom's paths through the woods have been restored and members of the Northenden community are acting as guides for visitors interested in exploring the rich variety of fauna and flora there. Helped by separate grants from Manchester Council the Friends restored the memorial stone which Edward Watkin erected 150 years ago in memory of his father. Inaccessible at the top of a slope, it had for many years been hidden in ivy and brambles and smothered by a dead tree, its lettering obscured. Yet the stone is a unique physical link between two Manchester Men who played a key role in the city's history in the nineteenth century. Now the vegetation has been cleared, the dead tree has been felled (but left as a natural habitat) and a Council grant has paid for a new path to be laid up to the stone. Three lecterns draw visitors' attention to the history of the place and its amenities. The activities of the Friends in Rose Hill Woods have been awarded two prizes to celebrate their work for the community. The woods have been rated as an outstanding Site of Biological Importance and now have regional status.

In 2019, the 200th year since Watkin was born, a national Watkin Society was formed to promote the Watkin story and to encourage research into Edward and Absalom's great achievements (and failures).

The year 2019 became the year of the plaques. Manchester City Council finally made some amends for their total neglect of one of their great citizens by erecting a plaque to commemorate him in Philips Park, one of the three Parks for the People created by him in 1846. It was unveiled by four descendants of Absalom and Edward. On his 200th birthday, 26 September 2019, Chiltern Railways, which manages London's Marylebone Station, put up a plaque in the station concourse to honour the man who built the London terminus of his Great Central Railway, the last main line into the capital until the first High Speed 1 train arrived in 1994 from Paris, using a tunnel under the English Channel next to the remains of Watkin's 1880 tunnel. It was over a century late.

The Nearly Man of Northenden has found another ninepence.

Index